What people are saying about this book:

"Easy A's was the best book I have ever read about getting better grades in school. It was fun and easy to read. It felt like it was written for me. After reading it and applying the concepts that Dr. Klusky recommended, I was amazed at how easy it was to pull my grades up. Every student should read this book." - *Jody Taylor, Student.*

"Easy A's helped me cut through all the superfluous nonsense and enabled me to receive an A on my first college paper." - *Seth Samuels, Student.*

"Before working with Dr. J. schooling seemed so complex. After working with him schooling became a lot easier. Now it's simple, do-able, and fun. I will always benefit from our work. - *Thea Samuels, Student.*

"As I read Easy A's: Winning the School Game I was struck by the clarity and simplicity of the book. Unlike any book I have read on the subject, it is written in such a straight forward manner that students of all ages can understand it and benefit from its contents. It is a book that filled me with the hope that my children and students could improve their ability to learn, get better grades, and have fun doing it. It is filled with graphic examples that immediately raised my son's self esteem. This alone far exceeded the price.

If you are an elementary, high school, college, or graduate student, a parent, educator, or life-long learner—you don't want to be without this book. I wish I had this book earlier in my educational journey. Thank heaven I have it now to help myself, my children, and my students." - *Sue Fisher, Mother, Educator, Writer.*

"At last I have something to recommend to the many students I see who are helplessly stumbling through a science course not knowing what's wrong or how to set things right. This book is a gold mine of very specific and practical suggestions for improving class performance." - *Ray Lutz , Professor of Chemistry, Portland State University.*

"An excellent book! An excellent resource! I recommend it to any student–high school to post graduate school. It makes the academic game understandable and winnable." - *Kent Snyder, J.D.*

"I've known Dr. Klusky for approximately 30 years, which is all his scholastic life. I always wondered how he did so well in school with so little apparent effort. After reading Easy A's I am pleased that he has been able to set down his methods in a concise, thoroughly readable, and clear blueprint for others to follow." - *Gilbert Witte, M.D.*

"Dr. Klusky's approach to learning is progressive and efficient. I wish I had these tools when I was in college." - *Mark Schulman, Musician, Producer, ESL Instructor.*

"Throughout the course of these chapters Dr. Klusky develops with continuous creation the adaptation of practical thought with the economy of time and space. He succeeds by contrasting our current educational dilemma with the habits of common humanity providing solutions that ultimately make us benignly curious about human truth." - *Christopher Caliendo, Composer.*

Easy A's: Winning the School Game
The guide that will change the way you approach education

EASY A's:

WINNING THE SCHOOL GAME

J. Ira Klusky, Ph.D.

Illustrated by Leslie Mellberg

UPTONE
Press
Portland, Oregon

EASY A's:

WINNING THE SCHOOL GAME

by J. Ira Klusky, Ph.D.

Published by:
Uptone Press
P.O. Box 82993
Portland, Oregon 97282

Publisher's Cataloging-in-Publication Data
Klusky, J. Ira
Easy A's: Winning the School Game
Includes Index.
1. Learning Skills. 2. Study Skills. 3. Academic
Achievement. 4. Self Management.
Library of Congress Catalogue Card Number: 92-61334
ISBN 0-9634011-6-5 $9.95 Softcover

Printed in the United States of America

I dedicate this book to my parents, who, through their love and smiles, laid the foundation for me to win the school game.

CONTENTS

Chapter 8 Relationships:
The Politics of Education   153

Chapter 9 College:
Getting In and Out With Style 171

ACKNOWLEDGEMENTS

Welcome to my favorite part of the book, for it is here I get to publicly thank all those who contributed to its creation.

This book would not have come to pass without the love, patience, and guidance of my friend and mentor, Jim Samuels. All the information in Chapter 2 (The Rules Of The Game), and much of the information in Chapter 3 (Creating Order From Chaos...) and Chapter 8 (Relationships: Mastering The Politics Of Education), was taken from his lectures. Jim also got the ball rolling on the art work. Many of the illustrations were taken from his original conceptions. In many more ways than these is this book a result of his spirit and genius, both of which are woven into its fabric.
Thank you, Jim.

Leslie Mellberg was responsible for fleshing out and manifesting those original conceptions, as well as contributing many of her own. For me, a great portion of this book's entertainment value is rooted in her wonderful illustrations. Having the opportunity to work with her was one of the high points of my writing experience.
Thanks, Leslie.

Kathy Chappelle, M.A., herself an educator, did a wonderful job editing this book, and taught me a lot of what I needed to know in order to write Chapter 7 (Writing for High Grades), She also provided me with much food for thought during our many discussions/arguments about public education.
Thanks, Kathy.

Susie Kobelin and Master Bruce Terrill took on the unenviable task of transcribing my attrociously hand written manuscript. That they succeeded at doing so as fast and accurately as they did is testament to their understanding and support.
Thanks, Susie and Master Terrill.

Mark and Sue Fisher trusted me and believed in this project enough to take a chance supporting it. I am humbled by such trust and belief.
Thanks, Mark and Sue.

My thanks also go to:
* Sasha Samuels for her much appreciated help with the cover layout and color coordination.
* Tony Mason and Ron Trevarthen, computer consultants extraordinaire, for all their technical support.
* Dr. Gilbert Witte, my friend since childhood, and the brightest student I have ever known, for his insights into the studenting process; Orcian though they may be.
* All my friends and fellow students at the Mentat School, Inc. for all your love, support, and sanity.
Thank you one and all.

Finally, a psychic thanks to the two students sitting in front of me in a Behavior Modification class at Portland State University in the winter of 1981, who, upon my over-hearing their description of all the work they did to prepare for a test we were about to take, first prompted me to ask the question: "Why do some students do all that work?"

"How you react will determine your existence"

Jim Samuels

CHAPTER 1

THE GAME

America is a country of bean counters! As a society we seem to care only about the bottom line. How much money did you make? How many widgets did you sell? Were profits up from last quarter? Can we make this product for less in Mexico? (So what if we strip our economy of another 10,000 jobs!) Can we fire John Smith, who makes $75,000/yr, and who has been with our company 20 years, and replace him with John Doe at half that salary? **We care more for the object—the dollar, the widget—than we do for the person.**

Unfortunately, this attitude not only drives our economy, it drives many facets of our society, and this includes our educational system. Much to the detriment of our students and their teachers, **our educational system is driven by the same bean counters that drive the rest of our society.** It is a system that defines success by the bottom line—high GPAs and Standardized Test Scores—rather than on knowledge and ability.

Want a job as lawyer? The higher the standing of your law school, and the higher your standing within that school, the more likely it is you will get the job you want. How do you get into such a highly ranked law school? Simple—attend a highly ranked college/university, graduate with a high GPA, and score extremely well on your LSAT (the standardized test for law school). How do you get into a highly ranked college? Easy—have a high GPA in an academic high school program and do extremely well on your SATs.

The same is true in medicine, clinical psychology, and business management—all fields in which you have to be adept at working with people. **All fields in which it is not uncommon for some of the best students (those with the highest GPAs and Test Scores) to make some of the worst professionals.** It is true of many professions.

Mind you, there are exceptions. If your family is wealthy enough to buy the school of your choice a library, you will likely be allowed to attend. If you are a Kennedy, a Bush, or otherwise well connected you will also likely be able to enroll in the school of your choosing. More important, **there are mavericks in every field, in every system.** There are men and women who base their evaluations of people on factors other than numbers, factors such as ability, potential, integrity, and character. They often will take chances on those with lesser numbers if they have the right combination of other qualities. More often than not these chances will work out to the benefit of all concerned.

This then is the essence of our educational/economic system: **regardless of your depth of knowledge, level of ability, or amount of desire, the greatest opportunities go to those with the best numbers—the best bottom line.**

The purpose of this book is to provide you with the tools necessary to excel at this game, to the best of your ability, in the most efficient way possible—to get the highest grades with the least effort, all the while having as much fun as you can.

If some of you bridle at this approach—Good! **Maybe we can do something to make it obsolete.** Don't hold your breath, though. I agree that in the best of lands a love of learning and child-like wonder so commonly found in young children would be nurtured, and like these young children our students would love to learn for learning's sake. In this land, schools would promote such motivation and encourage the personal expression of such an ideal. Grades would not exist because students would not need to be either evaluated or motivated in such a callous manner. Students would learn happily.

Unfortunately, we do not live in this land. We live in a land of bean counters who worship the bottom-line, and **this bottom line mentality has distorted the educational process for us as students.** The quest for grades often kills our love of learning at a young age. We are taught learning for the sake of learning is not enough. We see this attitude reflected in the eyes of our parents and teachers. We come to know it as we are rewarded for good grades and punished for poor ones. **School becomes simply a means to an end.** While a college degree no longer guarantees us a good paying job, it is almost impossible to get one without holding such a degree.

This bottom line mentality also has distorted the educational process for our teachers. Teachers have to spend so much time grading and justifying those grades to students and parents, as well as administrators, that their is little time left for generating creative, stimulating lesson plans. Students ask teachers to defend their grading system rather than the applicability of Shakespeare to modern life. Teachers spend more time discussing points than they do discussing pointillism..

This is simply the reality of the world in which we find ourselves. **So long as the game is run by the bean counters your success at the game will be determined by your ability to play by their rules and the bottom line.** I promise if the rules change, I will write another book. However, for the time being, if you want to have the best chance to win the school the game, you need to be competent using the skills and attitudes laid out in this book. So let the game begin!

WINNING THE SCHOOL GAME

To win the school game you will need to be competent at five basic groups of skills:

* **You need to be able to control your space, your time, and your attention**
* **You need to accurately determine what is and what is not going to be on tests**
* **You need to be able to put information in your mind and easily get it back out again**
* **You need to be able to take tests for high scores**
* **You need to be able to write papers**

To win the school game you also need to be competent at utilizing two viewpoints:

* **You need to be a student of the game as well a student in the classroom**
* **You need to be a strategist**

As a student you need to get used to seeing the world as your teachers see it (Not forever—only for a time. When you're through being a student you can move back into your own world view). **You need to be able to see the real rules of the system you're in, not just the rules your teachers and administrators want you to follow.** You need to understand how the system really works.

As a strategist **you need to be able to plot and scheme** (you know—plan, organize your efforts, look for short-cuts). **You need to understand the politics of your school, and use them to your advantage.**

Finally, and of greatest import, **you need to have the desire to win.** For while it is true that most of you can improve your grades, get into and graduate from the schools you want, and have more free time, **gaining competency with the skills and viewpoints necessary to do so will take time and energy—** more at first then less as you progress. With practice these skills will become easy for you to apply. It will be your desire that will take you through the initial stages.

USING THE BOOK — STUDENTS

This book is set up to provide you with the tools necessary to master the skills and viewpoints you will need to play the school game to the best of your ability. Though there is a certain logic to the order of the chapters, and I believe it best to read it straight through, it is not necessary that you read this book cover to cover. You may skim the chapters to get an idea what they are about, then read the parts that interest you most. However you decide to use this book is up to you—it's your book.

In many of the chapters you will find exercises. **Do the exercises. They will help you master the skills you need.** If they seem simple—Good! They are meant to be. If some of them seem trite or useless—they are the ones you probably need to do the most. Do them. Do all the exercises and see what happens. They are actually fun once you get into them. And you might be surprised at some of the results.

EXPECTATIONS

What can you expect from this book? It mostly depends on your desire to improve and where you are when you start applying the skills put forth on the following pages. **In general, the more you work at mastering these skills, the greater gain you'll see.** If you read this book and do not practice any of the exercises or change any of your views, you will essentially be unchanged, and can expect to do as well as you did before you picked up this book. **If you work and become competent with the skills in this book you can expect either your grades to improve, your work time to decrease, or both.**

Where you're starting from is also important in determining what you can expect. Students getting C's do not ordinarily start getting A's overnight, unless of course the C's are only the result of out-and-out laziness. It will usually take less time to consistently get A's if you started out getting B's than if you started out getting C's. I firmly believe **almost any student currently getting D's can get C's, almost any student getting C's can get B's, and almost any student currently getting B's can get A's by simply improving their approach to their schooling.** I also believe that if one's desire is strong enough, almost anyone can eventually consistently get A's.

USING THE BOOK — TEACHERS

Optimally, the skills set forth in this book would be integrated into our students' education from day one so that by the time they get to middle school strong, effective learning habits would be set. Since habits are going to be established one way or the other, we might as well help them establish habits that work.

Contrary to what some say, this does not require a complete overhaul of lesson plans, nor does it require drastically changing a curriculum. **This can be done by tailoring assignments to reflect the habits we most want them to develop.** For example, instead of simply assigning a chapter as a reading assignment, you can have students generate an outline of the chapter. When teaching multiplication tables, you can have them design their own flashcards then test themselves or each other. Of greatest import in this process is letting the students know **why** they are doing such assignments—how such assignments fit into the big picture. Often a teacher will create a wonderful exercise for her particular subject, one that really gets at learning skills, and one that her students enthusiastically perform. The only thing missing is that the students never realize that such an exercise can also be used to learn material in other classes as well.

The concept of learning by creating one's own questions and answering them can easily be presented to first graders. The fundamentals of good studenting can be presented to fourth and fifth graders. I have taught the Levels of Learning to sixth graders while I taught them how to flashcard.

By the time most students reach the seventh grade their study and learning habits are set. It is frightening that before this time most students have never had any learning skills training, and those that have, more often than not, either do not recall it or do not use much of what they were taught. Changing habits once they are entrenched is a monumental task, a task that has almost zero chance of success without a lot of activity.

Therefore, **if you are using this book for a learning skills class, make certain that your students do the exercises.** If you have the time, give them ample opportunity to master them and integrate them into their study routines. I have found it most beneficial to have my students use the classes they are taking at the time I teach them as their own workshop. They can use notes they have taken for flashcarding and books they are reading for outlining. They will learn best if you make what you teach as meaningful to their immediate circumstances as you can. Also, please have your students create ways to apply these skills to all of their classes.

If you are not specifically teaching a learning skills class and would like to integrate this material into your own lesson plans, adjust your assignments to reflect the skills you want your students to develop. If you are creative, you can come up with all manner of ways to help your students increase their skill level, while you reduce the time you have to spend grading. If you can, get your fellow teachers to do the same. **Optimally an entire school would have a coherent and consistent skill development policy that would provide its students with the means to establish new and improved habits of study.**

USING THE BOOK — PARENTS

I believe most parents truly want to help their children succeed. I also believe that when it comes to education, many parents do not have the skills necessary to provide effective help and rapidly become frustrated. **This book will provide you with tools you can use to help your children reach their educational goals.**

If your children are in high school, **you and they will get the most out of this book if you sit down and work through it together.** If they are in middle or junior high school, you will most likely need to work through it with them. If they are in elementary school, read through the book, pick out lessons that you feel apply to their present situation, and teach them. A good place to start is by teaching them how to create their own work space (Chapter 3). As they progress through school and require new skills, teach them. **If you take the time to understand the material in this book, you will be able to provide valuable support for your sons and daughters throughout their education.**

LEARNING AND GETTING GOOD GRADES

Learning and getting good grades are two different, though sometimes overlapping, activities. As such they require somewhat different sets of skills. **More often than not, learning is self-directed.** Learning is usually motivated by interest on the part of the learner. When we learn something we decide what it is we want to learn, and the depth at which we want learn it. If you are interested in music and wish to write songs, you may do so by sitting at a piano and working, hit or miss. You may instead find song writers and learn from them. You also may go to a school and take music theory and poetry writing classes. If you really want to learn to write songs, **you will find an approach that works best for you and spend as much time and energy as you can muster to learn what you need to know.**

Getting good grades is different. **Getting good grades is most often other-directed.** A teacher will tell you what you need to learn, how well you need to learn it, and often how you will go about learning it. We need to measure up to someone else's standards. While we are interested in the end result, a high school diploma, a college degree, a Ph.D., often we are not interested in the particular subject at hand. **Getting good grades is an end-result-oriented process. It involves determining what information is important and how to best present that information.**

Learning and getting good grades overlap when you are interested in both the subject and the end result. Learning can be a difficult proposition without the necessary skills, even when your interest in the subject is high. Learning when you are absolutely not interested in the subject and have not mastered those skills is almost impossible. **At the core of this book are those skills and attitudes necessary for both successful learning and getting good grades. If you master them you'll find both learning and getting good grades easier.** You will be better at getting the grades you want in areas that hold little interest for you, and you will be better at learning the material you find interesting.

I have three wishes for all of you. I wish that you master the skills and attitudes presented in this book you have begun to explore. I wish that you get the grades you want, that you get into and graduate from the programs and schools of your choice. Most of all, I wish that in the land of the bean counters you find fun and success.

CHAPTER 2

THE RULES
OF THE GAME

The purpose of this chapter is to clarify some basic concepts. It is very important that you understand them before you move on. This chapter is organized into three sections. The first section defines some fundamental principles. Learn these. Your ability to succeed is based on your understanding of them. The more complete your understanding, the greater the chance you will do well. The second section discusses the stages we all move through on our way to mastery of any skill. These stages are called the "Levels of Learning." The final section discusses the viewpoint of the *STUDENT*, the attitude that will be the foundation for all our subsequent work.

DEFINITIONS

UNDERSTAND:

Literally, "to stand under." To grasp the meaning of.

To understand something **you have to make it more important than yourself.** You have to "stand under" it. If you want to truly understand another's viewpoint, you must let their viewpoint dominate your thinking—at least for a time. Once you fully understand their way of thinking, not only are you free to agree or disagree with their position, you are more able to do so intelligently. For example: you are in a Biology class and your teacher says "The sole purpose of all life is to reproduce itself." You strongly disagree. You happen to think life has many purposes, some even higher than reproduction. To argue for your viewpoint convincingly, you need to know why your teacher holds her viewpoint. That is, you need to see life the way she sees it. Only then will you be able to identify the strengths and weaknesses of her position, dissect it, and make a strong case for your own view.

LEARN:

1a) To gain knowledge or understanding of, or skill in, by study instruction or experience.
1b) To acquire (as a skill or habit or modification of an existing habit) through experience, practice, or exercise.

The important point here is that **the one gaining the knowledge, skill or understanding is the one doing the learning.** The learner is the one that changes. This will make more sense when we define the roles of the teacher and the student. If you learn the skills presented in this book, you will be changed. Regarding these skills, you are the learner.

STUDY:

The application of the mental faculties to the acquisition of knowledge.

Studying is one of the prime ways we learn. In our American school system it is the chief way we learn.

STUDENT:

A person engaged in study; one devoted to learning.

The roles of a student are to study and to learn. Granted, some teachers make learning easier while others make it more difficult, and still others make it all but impossible. Regardless of the quality of your teachers **you are responsible for your own learning.** Whether or not you learn something and how well you learn it are up to you. Remember, the one who learns is the one who changes. The student is the one who changes.

TEACHER:

One who instructs.

Instruct: To give special knowledge or information to.

Teachers provide the knowledge; students learn it. **Teachers are responsible for the quality of the knowledge they provide as well as the quality of the method by which they provide it. Teachers are not responsible for students learning—Students are!** If you, the student, have not learned what you need to know well enough, it is your responsibility to go somewhere or to someone for help. This may simply mean paying more attention in class, or it may mean talking to your teacher, your advisor, a friend, or perhaps even another teacher.

The teacher/student interaction is pretty straightforward. It is the teacher's job to present his or her students with new viewpoints, new ways of looking at the world. It is the student's job to take these viewpoints and understand them. Then, after these viewpoints are understood, it is the student's responsibility to evaluate which ones are valuable, and how those valuable views may best be integrated into the student's life (Samuels, 1990). Let's go back to the previous Biology example. The teacher provides a new viewpoint—"The sole purpose of life is to reproduce itself"—and she gives her reasons. It is each student's job to understand her view, then to evaluate that view for him or herself, being free to agree, disagree, agree in part, etc. Why must you, the student, understand the viewpoint of the teacher? Simple, that's the viewpoint the teacher will be evaluating and testing you on. While it's possible to disagree with a teacher's viewpoint and still earn a good grade, to do so you must have an excellent understanding of what you're disagreeing with.

READY OR NOT (Samuels 1983)

The following are five factors that will greatly influence the success you will have as a student in a given study session (this includes class time). For best results you should:

BE * RESTED	You need to be adequately rested in order to perform at your best. Not being adequately rested is a stress factor and will decrease your effectiveness.
HAVE * EATEN	You need to be adequately fed in order to perform at your best. Being hungry or improperly fed is a stress factor and will also decrease your effectiveness.
BE * ALCOHOL FREE	Alcohol is another stress factor. This should be obvious. Generally speaking if you've had alcohol within the last 24 hours, your abilities will be limited.
BE * DRUG FREE	This one should also be fairly obvious. It takes about six weeks for our bodies to be free of the effects of many drugs. Being under the influence of drugs will also put a strain on your system.

While you can and sometimes have to function under less than ideal conditions, it pays to have an idea of what you can expect from yourself so you can make the appropriate adjustments. The fifth factor is your level of commitment:

* <u>Y</u>OUR READINESS

> Are you ready to be a student? Are you ready to put your opinions aside, and take and experience the views of the instructor. If you are not, the chances of you learning anything are slim. If you are, you can learn just about anything.

In your interaction with this book, I am the teacher and you are the student. I am going to ask you to do things that may be unfamiliar to you. I am also going to ask you to take viewpoints you might not ordinarily take. If you are a parent, a teacher, or an administrator, some of these might directly conflict with views you have previously held dear. To all who are reading: be prepared to experience something new.

Are you READY? Are you properly rested? Answer the question! Really! Answer the question!! Have you eaten? Have you had any alcohol in the last 24 hours? Have you had any drugs in the last 6 weeks? Are you ready to be a student?

(Here's a clue—If you haven't answered these questions, you are not ready to be a student. If this is the case, either get your act together and be a student or put the book down until you are ready!)

GO ON, ANSWER THE QUESTIONS!

IF YOU'RE READY, LET'S CONTINUE

THE LEVELS OF LEARNING   (Samuels, 1982)

The levels of learning are four stages we all go through when we learn new skills. As you will be learning new skills throughout this book, understanding these levels will help you better assess your progress. There are four levels of learning:

1. Unconscious Incompetence
2. Conscious Incompetence
3. Conscious Competence
4. Superconscious Competence

LEVEL 1: UNCONSCIOUS INCOMPETENCE

This is the first stage of learning. **At this stage you are unaware (unconscious) that you cannot perform a skill (you are incompetent).** Unconscious incompetence takes two forms. In the first, you are unaware a particular skill exists and therefore are incompetent at it. At this moment many of you are unconsciously incompetent in this way with respect to many of the skills in this book.

The second form of unconscious incompetence occurs when you think you can perform a skill and you in fact cannot. Some of you will experience this mode of unconscious incompetence a little later in the book when I describe a particular technique (e.g., post-testing) and you assert you can do it without ever having demonstrated the ability. Remember, you are incompetent at a skill until you actually can perform it consistently. The question at this level is whether or not you are aware you are incompetent. The simplest and fastest way to graduate to the next level of learning is to accept that you are, in fact, incompetent with respect to a certain skill.

LEVEL 2: CONSCIOUS INCOMPETENCE

This is the second stage of the learning process and in some respects it can be the most fun. At this level **you are aware (conscious) that you cannot perform a particular skill (you are incompetent).** This level is so wonderful because it is the level necessary to begin the learning process. Also, since you are incompetent, it's not only OK to make mistakes—it's expected! So, relax and learn. The way you move through this level to the next (conscious competence) is to **become more and more aware of how you make your mistakes.** The more clearly you understand how you make your mistakes, the more apparent and simpler the corrections are! Once you've made all the necessary corrections, and can perform the skill correctly and consistently, you graduate to the third level of learning.

LEVEL 3: CONSCIOUS COMPETENCE

At this stage **you can consistently perform a skill (you are competent) when you are paying attention (conscious).** Remember, you only graduate to this level once you have demonstrated that you can perform a skill correctly and consistently. To graduate to the final learning stage, you have to practice that skill until you master it, and you have to practice it perfectly. You know the old saying "practice makes perfect"? Well, it's not quite accurate. What is true is "**perfect practice makes perfect.**" You have to practice a skill correctly in order to master it. When you have mastered it, you have reached the fourth and final level of learning.

How do you know when your practice is correct? Your practice is correct if you are showing improvement. In the "school game," if your grades are getting better, your work is getting easier, and/or your confidence is growing—you're on the right track. You're practicing correctly.

LEVEL 4: SUPERCONSCIOUS COMPETENCE

At the fourth stage you are very aware (superconscious) that you can perform a skill (you are competent). When you are superconsciously competent, **you perform a skill so well that it has become a natural part of you.**

Let's take a very simple example to illustrate how all of us proceed through these levels of learning. We will use the skill of tying shoes. At some time when you were an infant you did not even know that "tying shoes" existed and of course, you couldn't do it. You were unconsciously incompetent (learning level 1).

At some point, perhaps when you were three, you noticed your mom tying your shoes and tried to do it yourself. You jumbled your laces together, went to her and said, "Mommy, I tied shoes!" You were still unconsciously incompetent because you still could not tie your shoes and didn't know you couldn't. Mom told you you didn't really tie them, so you asked her to teach you.   You had moved to the next stage: you were consciously incompetent (learning level 2).

Then you started practicing. At first all you knew was that every time you tried, you failed. Later, you began to see how you failed: you noticed you weren't wrapping one lace around the loop of the other properly. You were becoming more aware of how you were incompetent.   You are moving through conscious   incompetence   and   approaching   conscious competence. One day you actually tied your own shoes. You were very pleased with yourself. You were now at the top end of conscious incompetence. The next time you tried to tie your shoes, you missed again. You also missed the next time. The time after that you did it right. It was hit-and-miss for a while. The hits began to accumulate and soon you were doing it right just about every time. You were then consciously competent at tying your shoes (learning level 3). You still needed to pay lots of attention, and when you did, you succeeded.

After a few more months of practice, tying your shoes became second nature to you. You did it right every time with little thought. You became superconsciously competent at tying your shoes (learning level 4).

I understand tying shoes is a fairly mundane skill for most of us. However, if we are to master a set of skills, we must proceed through the same four stages. Please understand that few humans become superconsciously competent at substantial skills (mastery of a musical instrument or of accounting, for instance). To do so requires much time and work, and most of us are not that motivated. Fortunately it does not take becoming superconsciously competent with the skills presented here to succeed at school. Conscious competence is enough. If you become consciously competent with the skill of being a student you will be well on you way to a smooth, successful, and fun scholastic experience. To do so will simply require your time and attention.

THE FASTEST ROUTE TO SUCCESS

The fastest, most effective method for becoming competent at any skill is to find someone who is successful at what you want to do and copy them. That's right—copy them. Why?

Simple. If you copy someone who is already successful, you will benefit from all their learning, all their experience. You can bypass years, if not decades, of wasted time and energy doing the trial-and-error learning this person has already done. So, if you want to be a carpenter, find a good one and ask if you can study with him/her. If you want to be a graphic artist, find a successful one and see if s/he will take you under their wing. If you want to excel in marketing, find someone who is accomplished in that arena and do everything related to marketing exactly the way s/he does it.

This is called the Mentor/Apprentice relationship. It is one of the most powerful relationships a person can be involved in. It is the way successful men and women have learned their trades for thousands upon thousands of years. **It is a relationship in which the mentor, in exchange for something of value (usually work), agrees to teach the apprentice what s/he knows about their area of expertise.** Not only does the apprentice benefit from the mentor's knowledge, the apprentice benefits from the mentor's connections, which can often be even of greater value.

In return, the apprentice must provide something of value for the mentor. To find out what you can do in exchange for your mentor's guidance—ask. If you can come to an agreement that works for both of you—great. If not, find a mentor with whom such an agreement can be arranged.

THE *STUDENT*

What is a *STUDENT*? A *STUDENT* is a person in school with a particular approach to learning. To get an idea of what being a *STUDENT* really is all about, think of someone you greatly admire—even idolize—in a field that you're interested in. If you're interested in acting, think of your favorite actor or actress, maybe D. Hoffman or M. Streep. If you're interested in writing, think of the writer you most look up to, perhaps Hemingway or Faulkner. If you're into physics; you may think of Einstein or Hawking. If you're into football or basketball, you might consider Montana or Magic. You get the idea. Whatever your area of interest, take a moment and make sure you have a particular person in mind. Got somebody? Good.

Now, imagine going to that person and asking him or her to teach you all they know about their field, and imagine them agreeing to do so. Imagine how you would respond to them as your teacher/mentor. You would likely be a little in awe, extremely attentive, and amazingly cooperative. If your mentor suggested you look at a particular problem a particular way— you would do so without hesitation. If he or she told you to practice a particular exercise—you would do so with gusto. If you can imagine what such a relationship would feel like, you can get a feel for what being a *STUDENT* is all about. **It is an incredibly powerful position—a position most people will never experience.** It is a position from which you can learn and grow at an astounding rate. It is a position best expressed by these 5 tenets:

A- Aim: Know it !
W- Whatever is necessary: Do it !
A- Attention: Focus it !
R- Responsibility: Take it !
E- Enjoy yourself: Have fun !

* AIM: KNOW IT!

First you need to have **some sense of where you are going.**
It is of great benefit to know why you are in school. If you are
there because you want to be a lawyer, engineer, teacher,
writer, physicist, etc.—great! If you are there because you just
want a degree—great! If you are there because you have to
be—great! **What matters is that you know why you are there.**
The more clear you are about where you are going, the easier it
will be to adapt your current schoolwork to your future work.
For example, if you are in a college program that requires a
senior thesis (or for that matter if you are in high school and
expect to be in such a college program), and if you know the
subject area of that thesis (English history, for instance), you
can gear a lot of your work towards that thesis. If you are in a
college social psychology class you can study the social
psychology of the English people. If you're in a high school
world studies class and have to write a paper you can write it
on England's history. This brings to mind one of the more fun
games to play. For how many different classes can you use the
same paper? (More on this later.)

Remember to **do as much work as you can with an eye
toward your future work.** You're going to have to do the work
anyway—why not make it count for as much as possible?

* WHATEVER IS NECESSARY: DO IT!

In the early 1970s, Bruce Lee, a master martial artist and the
creator of Jeet Kun Do, appeared on a television talk show in
China with other master martial artists, all representing
different schools and styles. One of the guests, a master of
Aikido, was demonstrating one of the fundamental skills of his
art, "Ki training." He did so by standing at the center of the

stage and inviting others to move him (he was approximately 5'4", 120 lbs.). Many people tried, including some very large weight-lifter types. They tried to lift him, push him, and pull him. All failed. It was a very impressive demonstration. After about 6 or 7 minutes, Master Lee asked if he might try. He walked up to the Aikido master and pushed on him. The master didn't budge. He pulled on him. The master still didn't budge. Then Master Lee stepped back and gave him a powerful kick to his face. The Aikido master went flying across the stage. The audience was hushed, the host looked embarrassed, and before taking his seat Master Lee said, "In my style we do whatever is necessary to accomplish the goal."

Doing whatever is necessary to accomplish the goal is one of the primary attitudes of the successful student. If your goal is to get into a quality four-year college, there are always ways in. Some are more direct than others. The simplest most direct way is to have a 4.0 GPA in high school and score over 1500 on your SATs.

"Not many of us will do that," you say.

"Fine," I say. "A 3.2 GPA and 1200 on your SATs should do it too."

"Yeah, yeah," you say. "But I blew it in high school. I worked hard, yet only managed a 2.5 GPA and only got a 900 on my SATs."

This does make it tougher. You will likely have to go to a junior college, work more effectively and—more importantly—work smarter than you did in high school, in order to pull a GPA that will allow you to transfer to a good four-year school. Or, perhaps you can find a teacher that will help you write a major college-level, thesis-type paper and submit to the Dean of the college you want to attend to demonstrate that you can successfully do college work. (If you do the paper correctly, you should be able to adapt parts of it to fit the writing requirements of 3 to 5 other classes). If you have the will, there is always a way. A *STUDENT* **finds that way. This attitude is the essence of being a** *STUDENT*.

Be aware, when "doing whatever is necessary" it is important to limit your choice of actions to those that are legal as well as in harmony with your own morality. I don't know of anything on this planet that is worth the price of your soul. All the other options you can think of are yours for the choosing.

* ATTENTION: FOCUS IT !

The *STUDENT* **works until the goal is accomplished.** Optimally, there isn't that much work. Sometimes there is. It depends on your goal and your approach. You want an A in geometry. Great! You bombed your first test? OK. All that means is that your approach was wrong.   Keep paying attention until you find an approach that works. Ask for help from friends, parents and teachers.   Check out other books. Whatever it takes, **keep your attention focused.**

And what do you focus your attention on? You focus it on whatever will help you get what you want. Does the teacher talk more slowly when she's going over material that will be on the test? Does she write anything on the blackboard? Does she repeat the items that she feels are important? Do your friends have any simple methods for understanding and remembering material? *STUDENTS* pay attention to anything that will help them improve their grades or make it easier to get the grades they've been getting. **They keep paying attention until they have achieved their objective.**

* RESPONSIBILITY: TAKE IT !

It's that simple. **You are responsible for your own education!** I've said it before and I'll say it again. You are responsible for your own education! The *STUDENT* knows and understands this. Your chances of success will increase in direct proportion to the amount of responsibility you accept. What does this mean? It means that no matter what happens in or out of class you take the viewpoint that your grades are your responsibility. You assume **the grades you get are not the teacher's fault, the school's fault, your friend's fault, nor your family's fault. They are your fault.** If **you** get a D in history, it's not because the teacher was terrible, it's because **you** paid enough attention and did what was necessary to get that D. If **you** get an A in chemistry, it is not because you had a good teacher; it is because **you** paid enough attention and did what was necessary to get that A.

Many factors contribute to your performance. We all know that bad teachers make it harder and good teachers make it easier to do well, just as having a bad family life will make your education rougher and a good one will make it smoother. For many of us it is all too easy to blame outside factors on the results we achieve. While this may make us feel better, the costs of this are severe. The more you place the blame for a grade or a test score on outside factors, the more impotent, powerless, you become. After all, if your grades are a result of bad teaching, what hope is there for you to improve your grade? You have no choice other than accepting C's or D's. It's not your fault. Do you see where this leaves you? Powerless. Impotent. Assuming responsibility will restore your power.

So, whether you have it hard or easy, rough or smooth, the *STUDENT's* bottom line is: **Did you do the work necessary to get the grade you want?** If you did—good going! If you did not—get to work! The tools in this book will help you. It is your responsibility to become consciously competent at applying these tools to your own work. If you take on this responsibility you will almost certainly improve!

* ENJOY YOURSELF: HAVE FUN !

Fun is great! Fun is what motivates us! When we get right down to it—if it isn't fun we don't want anything to do with it. My Mentor once summed up the game of life this way: "The person who dies with the biggest grin on his face—wins!" For most of us, fun is what matters most. **As you move through life, it is important that you enjoy yourself.**

One of the things that is really great about fun is that there are actually two kinds of fun: **short-term fun and long-term fun. When you're planning your fun you need to take both into account. This is critical!** It can't be emphasized enough! **You need to plan your fun so that the fun you have in the short-term sets you up for greater fun in the long-term.** If all a person does is have short-term fun, without regard for their future, that person is setting him/herself up for a world of pain in the long-term. If a person has no fun at all in the short-term, that person is probably in a world of hurt already.

You have to take both into account. Partying is great fun. However, if you go out and party until you are so sick you have to stay in bed for three days just to recover—you killed off three days worth of opportunities to have fun. The same is true of your education. If you don't take care of business now—you seriously diminish your chances for having fun in the future. Your best bet is to be smart about your fun. **Take care of business now to set up your long-term fun, and make sure you're having fun as you do it.**

So remember to have fun! Discover ways to make school work enjoyable! Reward yourself for work well done. As important as it is to do what is necessary to accomplish your goals, it is equally important to have fun doing it. One of the many ways to do this is by rewarding yourself. Learn to enjoy the fruits of your labor. Make sure you have time for play. The *STUDENT* knows that in the long run **work and play are both important.**

REFERENCES

Samuels, J. S. (1982). Your personal power. Portland, OR: The Mentat School, Inc.

Samuels, J. S. (1983). Sorting it out. Portland, OR: The Mentat School, Inc.

Samuels, J. S. (1990). On being a student. Unpublished Lecture.

CHAPTER 3

CREATING ORDER FROM CHAOS:

MASTERING SPACE,
TIME, AND ECONOMICS

An old Steve Martin joke goes something like this:

"You know for the past year I've been doing a lot of growth-oriented work, attending workshops, seminars, lectures; and the one thing all of them have in common is their focus on goals. They all say we should set goals for ourselves and our goals should be set on gradients, one step at a time, each step slightly bigger than the previous one. For example, if your long-range goal is to run a marathon, make your first goal to run a mile, your next, 2 miles, then 5 miles, then 10 miles, then 15 miles, then 20 miles and then the marathon. Well, I took their advice to heart and started working on my goals, keeping in mind the importance of gradients. After much soul searching and exploring I finally came up with goals that are right for me. First I want to become master of all time, space, and dimension. Then I want to go to France."

Myself and many others found this to be a very funny bit (if you did not, imagine Steve Martin delivering it. If this doesn't work, all I can say is "you had to be there"). While he meant this to be a joke, there is some truth to it. In order for him to get to France, he would have had to have mastered at least a little bit of space, time, and dimension. Likewise with getting grades. To get good grades you have to have gained some control over your space, time, and (for our purposes) economics. To get straight A's you have to have gained a lot of control of space, time, and economics. In this chapter we are going to focus on what you must do to gain control of these. For many of you, that's going to mean changing some of your habits.

CHANGING HABITS

DIRECTION

One of the purposes of this book is to provide you with the opportunity to develop better studenting habits. The first thing you need in order to change a habit is direction. **Know what you are changing from and what you are changing to.** You need to know where you are and where you're going. You need to be conscious of your incompetence with the new behavior you want to establish (knowing where you are), and you need to be conscious of what competent behavior is (knowing where you are going). For example, take hitting a baseball or softball. You notice that you have a habit of taking your eye off the ball when you are at bat. You need to know the action you want to establish—keeping your eye on the ball—and the mistake you're currently making of taking your eyes off the ball. If you do not know your mistake, you will not think to change it. If you do not know the correct action, you will not know what to change to.

SUPPORT

The second thing you need in order to change your habits is support. You need people who are going to help you develop the habits you want and you need to ask them to do so. It is a major blunder to expect others to know what you're doing and give you support. You need to **let those close to you know what you're doing and ask for their support.** Although some of us can change our behavior on our own, it is often much easier to do so with the help of our family and friends.

Typically, you may seek support from your parents, other members of your family, teachers, and/or friends. If you want support and are having difficulty getting it, start supporting others. Do this by finding out about what they want, and doing whatever you can do to help them get it. The more support you put out, the more you will receive.

A note to parents and teachers: provide your children/students with as much support as you can. Be sure to give them plenty of validation when they do what they want to do correctly. When you check up on them, remember: you are supporting them—they are making these changes for their own betterment.

EXERCISES

This next series of exercises is designed to help you identify the best times and places for you to study.

Exercise 3.1 Where do you study?

a) List all the places where you have studied.

b) On a scale of 1 to 5, rate the amount of time you have spent studying in each of these places during the past quarter or semester.

1 = *very little*
2 = *a little*
3 = *moderate*
4 = *much*
5 = *very much*

Example:

Place	Time spent studying there (1 -5)
1. Desk in my room	5
2. Library	2
3. Friend's house	3
4. On the bus	1

Exercise 3.2 When do you study?

a) List the times during the day when you are most likely to study.

b) Use same scale as in ex. 3.1 (above), rate the amount of time you tend to use these times to study.

Example:

Time	Time spent studying there (1-5)
1. 3-4 p.m.	3
2. 4-5 pm	2
3. 5-6 pm	4
4. 6-7 pm	1

Exercise 3.3 What do you do when you're studying?

The next few times you sit down to do schoolwork, keep a log or record of what you actually do. Record your actions, then total up the time you actually studied. (If you really want to be hard-core, have someone who supports you keep a record on you also.)

Here's a typical example:

8:00pm	Sat down to study
8:01pm	Turned on radio
8:02pm	Got a snack
8:05pm	Opened book & read
8:20pm	Answered phone & talked to friend
8:30pm	Resumed reading
8:42pm	Just caught myself daydreaming
	(probably for 5 min.)
8:44pm	Read
8:50pm	Thought about girlfriend/boyfriend
8:52pm	Got another snack
8:55pm	Resumed reading
9:00pm	Stopped studying

Total Time: 60 minutes
Time Spent Studying: 31 minutes

Many students find just by deciding to do Exercise 3.3 they improve their concentration and efficiency. It can really be embarrassing/eye opening to become aware of what you're really doing. If you approach this exercise honestly it can be a lot of fun. Enjoy it and learn about yourself. When you have a better idea of where you're currently at in terms of how effectively you use your space, time, and attention, you can move on to thinking about how to better control them.

MASTERING SPACE

SOME THEORY

In the early academic literature on human learning and memory, much work was done on the effects of context on learning. Typically, it was found that recall is better for information tested in the space in which it was studied. This was called the "context effect." Taken to its extreme conclusion, for best results on a test, one should study in the exact place (down to the seat in which one will be sitting) and the exact time (e.g., 8-10am) that a test will be administered. This, of course, is impractical (though the image of a school full of students attempting to fulfill this prescription is a humorous one). However, the prescription that follows from this work is **consistency.** One should study in a usual place at some regular time. The logic is that that place and time will become enriched with associations of studying, learning, information, etc. and that this will contribute to one's efforts.

Later work in the field of human learning and memory revealed that information is best recalled if it is studied in a wide variety of places, the logic being that the information will get associated with many places, and therefore many varied sensations, hence the increased likelihood of some apparently arbitrary memory, or sensation facilitating recall of the pertinent information. The prescription that follows from this theory is that one should study in many places: one's home, the library, at school, on a bus, at a party, etc.

Which approach is best? A factor that the latter literature did not take into account is a place's conduciveness to concentration, concentration being a prime factor in the effectiveness of studying. I believe if one could concentrate effectively, studying in a variety of places is probably a better approach. However, it is a rare individual who can concentrate (i.e., place one's full attention on one subject) effectively at all for any significant length of time, even 5-10 minutes. It is therefore folly to believe that more than one in a thousand of us can concentrate as effectively on a bus as in a library, or in a park as at our homes. Given human nature and our propensity for dividing our attention, I am a strong proponent of the former approach.

WHERE TO STUDY

Study in a place in which you can concentrate most effectively (effectively concentrating involves placing all your attention on what you intend to place it on) **and study there consistently.** For most of us, this place will be quiet (visually as well as auditorally). If you're not sure where is the most effective place for you, do exercise 3.3 (*What do you do when you study*) in a variety of places and notice the results. It is important that at whatever place (there can be 2 or 3 different places if they're each truly effective) you choose, you do nothing other than schoolwork there. I'll say it again. **At the place of your choice, you only study.** If you decide your desk in your room is the best place for you to work, just work at your desk. If you get up to get a snack, eat it on your bed, in the kitchen—anywhere other than your desk. If you don't have a desk, pick a corner in your room and reserve that corner for studying.

This is the key to creating an excellent study environment. The effect of such an environment on your psyche can be enormous. **If you do it right you will have irresistible urges to work when you're in your place of study.** You want to condition your mind and body to go to work when you go to your selected place. That's why libraries are typically such good places to study. It is easier to think about schoolwork in a library than in most other places. Be creative in your choices. Some excellent *STUDENTS* have reported they get some of their best work done on public transportation. Experiment and find out what is best for you. **You know you have developed a good work space when you enter it and automatically start thinking of your studies. You know you have developed a great work space when you get those irresistible urges.** Look for these effects.

Exercise 3.4 Where do you concentrate most effectively?

Pick 3 different places and try out Ex. 3.3 .
(Page 31)

MASTERING TIME

SOME THEORY

I'd love to discuss theory, but to the best of my knowledge there are not any theories that are supported by any substantial evidence.

WHEN TO STUDY

Basically it's up to you. My main suggestion is that, like where you study, **you keep when you study as consistent as you can.** Are you a morning person? Work before class. An afternoon person? Work after class. An evening or late night type? Work then. It is important that you know when you truly work the best and arrange your time accordingly. Even so, if you pick any time and work consistently, your mind and body will adapt to that time. However, there are times that your mind and body more naturally like to work.

Exercise 3.5 When do you study most effectively?

Pick three different study times and see during which you get the most work done. Use the following 1-5 scale:

1 = None of what you planned to accomplish
2 = Less than half of what you planned to accomplish
3 = Half of what you planned to accomplish
4 = More than half of what you planned to accomplish
5 = All of what you planned to accomplish

SCHEDULING

The key to effective scheduling for most of us is having large enough blocks of time to get a substantial amount of our work accomplished. Whether you are aware of it or not this is how most of you actually work. If you tend to cram for tests or write papers the day or night before they're due, this is definitely your style. If you prefer to do smaller projects over shorter times, break up your assignments into manageable chunks and schedule your time accordingly. **Make your schedule fit your style.**

If you have a five-page book report to do and you know it will probably take 3 hours to do it, give yourself at least a 4-hour (or better, 5-hour) chunk of time in which to do it. Most people find if they sit down to work on a project all at once it can take them about 1/2 the time to get it done than if they did it 1 hour at a time. Your 7-hour term paper will likely take you 14 hours if you do it one hour at a time. I have included a typical weekly schedule of a student at Portland State University (see figure 1). (Note that this student took all of his classes on M,W,F so he could have large blocks of time to study, work, and play on T,Th,S. To help finance his schooling, he worked as a waiter in the evenings.)

There are many scheduling systems on the market (e.g., Daytimer). While most of them are very good, they tend to be more complex than most students need. If you currently enjoy using one of these organizing systems, please continue to do so. Most of you, however, do not use any on-going system so I will provide you one. I find it incredibly simple, effective and easy to use. All it requires is two pieces of paper, one for your weekly schedule (see figure 1), and the other for your semester or quarter schedule (see figure 2).

On the semester or quarterly schedule put down all test dates and dates that projects are due. This way you'll get a feel for the flow of the quarter or semester. On the weekly schedule, fill in your daily activities. Be sure to include out-of-school work time, play time, rest time, and free time. Most weeks your schedule will change a bit. So remember at some time during each week to plan your activities for the following week.

Figure 1: Sample Weekly Schedule

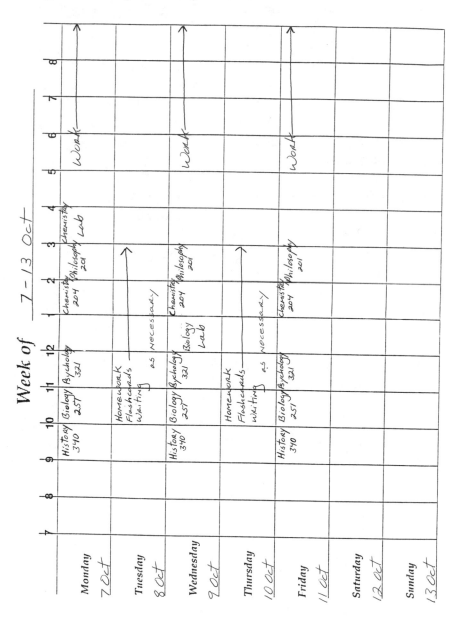

Figure 2: Sample Quarterly Schedule

October, 1991

S	M	T	W	T	F	S
29	30	1	2	3	4	5
6	7	8	9	10	11	12
13	14	15	16 *Chem Test 1*	17	18	19
20	21	22	23	24	25 *Bio Test 1*	26
27	28	29	30	31		

November, 1991

					1 *Phil Paper 1*	2
3	4 *Hist Mid-Term*	5	6 *Psych Mid-Term*	7	8	9
10	11	12	13	14	15 *Chem Test 2*	16
17	18	19	20 *Bio Test 2*	21	22	23
24	25	26	27	28	29	30

December, 1991

1	2 *Hist Paper*	3	4 *Chem Test 3*	5	6 *Bio Test 3*	7
8	9	10	11	12	13 *Phil Paper 2*	14
15	16 *Hist Final*	17 *Bio & Psych Finals*	18 *Chem Final*	19	20	21

HOW MUCH TIME SHOULD YOU STUDY?

How much time should I spend studying? Good question! The answer is, as much time as it takes to get the grade you need. Remember, when you take a test, even **if you need an A, you don't have to know everything!** You need to know about 90% of the material! If you simply need to pass you need to know 65-70% of the material. What this means is that you need to become aware of your state of readiness for a test. You need to develop a sense for what portion of the material you know. This is important because as you study you will reach a point of diminishing returns, a point after which the little knowledge you gain will not be worth the time it takes to acquire it.

Generally, every succeeding hour you study brings you less information. This is called diminishing returns. It works like this: the first two hours you study might bring you large amounts of information, the third hour, less, the fourth, even less and so on. Here is an hypothetical time/benefit scale for a hypothetical student with a psychology final to prepare for:

Amount of time studied		Percentage of the material known
0 hrs.	-	50%
1 hrs.	-	75%
2 hrs.	-	85%
3 hrs.	-	90%
4 hrs.	-	94%
5 hrs.	-	97%
6 hrs.	-	99%

If this student didn't study at all, she would expect to answer half of the questions on her final correctly. If she studied properly for an hour she might know three quarters of the material. If she studied for three hours she would likely get 90% on her final, enough for an A in most grading systems. In that three hours of studying she would have increased her score by 40%. If she studied yet another three hours she would only increase her score by 9%. This is what is meant by diminishing returns. Work beyond the first three hours i this situation is essentially wasted. This student would be much better off going to a movie!

Exercise 3.6 How much time do you need to study?

Keep track of the amount of time you study and the resulting grades.

TAKING CONTROL OF

YOUR SPACE AND TIME

PREPARING TO WORK

Before you begin your work, do all that you can to help yourself maintain your focus on your work. If you work at a desk, **only things that are directly related to the work you're doing should be on it.** Optimally, everything else should be put away in some orderly fashion. I know this might be asking a lot of some of you. Order may not be your style. If this is the case, you can throw everything off your desk and onto the floor, stuff it all in a drawer or toss it all in a closet. Out of sight, out of mind.

Next, **make sure that you are not disturbed.** If you're at home, put a sign on the door, ask someone in your family to take messages for you, and let them all know you are not to be disturbed. If you're living alone, **unplug the phone!!** (Note to parents: Support your sons and daughters by leaving them alone during their work. Protect them and their space. Only disturb them in case of extreme danger. You know: fire, earthquake, tornado.)

All that's now left for you to do before you begin working is to evaluate Your state of READYness: Rested, Eaten, Alcohol, Drugs, and taking your state into consideration, **set your goal for what you want to accomplish during this time period.** Your goal should meet three criteria:

1. **It should definitely move you toward your longer range goals (e.g., accomplishing it should increase your chances for an A)**
2. **It should be realistic (i.e., you should be able to accomplish it in the time you set for yourself),**
3. **If you do accomplish it you should feel a sense of satisfaction for a job well done**

Remember, goal setting is a skill, one at which many of you are incompetent. That's OK! Remember what this means. At first expect to make mistakes. Expect to set some goals that you can't accomplish, some that upon accomplishing will have felt too easy and others that are just right. Keep paying attention and you'll soon get competent at setting appropriate goals— goals at which you can succeed at and feel good about the success.

THE PROCRASTINATION KILLER   (Samuels, 1981)

Even after you have gotten control of your space and time, and after you have set your goals and are ready to work, some of you (perhaps many of you) will still not work. Your mind will wander, you'll pace the floor, you'll feel like calling a friend or getting something to eat. Perhaps you'll want to watch T.V., write a letter, or play with your cat. Anything but work. **At these times you are a procrastinator.** I'll bet most of you spend more time procrastinating than you actually do studying! Never fear. We have just the weapon for you. This weapon is perhaps the most deadly weapon in the entire arsenal contained in this book. It is so deadly, so utterly awesome, so bloody effective, that only a few of you will have the courage to try it, and only a few of those that do will succeed upon their first attempt. However, if you persist until you have successfully wielded this weapon you will likely have a profound experience, one that could change your life.

The procrastination killer was given to me by my Mentor, Jim Samuels, some of whose other teachings you will find in this book. I have since passed it on to hundreds of my students. Now I pass it on to you. Do you have courage to attempt it? Time will tell. Here it is. If you want to kill procrastination and greatly increase your ability to act on your goals, literally—**Shut Up and Just Do What Set Out To Do.**

Exercise 3.7 The Procrastination Killer

Once you have set your goal, BE SILENT UNTIL YOU HAVE ACCOMPLISHED YOUR GOAL.

It's that simple. Do not utter a word or sound until your goal is accomplished. Apply it on relatively small goals at first (book reports, flashcarding, reading and understanding book chapters). Once you have been successful at small tasks, apply the killer to larger tasks and see how quickly you get your work done. This killer is simple, direct, to the point, and most importantly—it works. See why you unplug the phone? You can help yourself by letting your friends and family know what you're doing and allowing them to support you. Or, you can have a fun time and simply do it and let anyone who tries to get your attention in on a unique experience. Either way, do it and move yourself. Good luck and may the force be with you.

MASTERING ECONOMICS:

MAKING TIME FOR ALL

THE THINGS YOU REALLY WANT TO DO

Economics is the science that deals with the production, distribution, and consumption of limited resources. Simply put, economics involves learning how to control limited resources. The resources you the *STUDENT* have to control are your time, space, and attention.

Know that **the school system is set up so it is not really possible to do all the work you're assigned in the manner your teachers expect you to do it.** This becomes increasingly true as you progress from high school to college to graduate school. In high school it is a rare student that does all the work. In college it is rarer still, and anyone that does probably doesn't have a life. In graduate school it is impossible. (Most graduate students don't have lives and they still can't do all the work!) Remember our discussion on short- and long-term fun? Don't worry! The system is also set up so that it's very possible to get A's and not do all the work. **While you don't need to do all the work, you do need to do the right work.** You need to do the work necessary to get the grade you want.

For now, let's talk about how best to use the time and attention you do have. Your time and attention are limited. That's just the way it is. If you have the necessary amount of time and attention to get the grades you want—great! If you do not, or would rather use your resources for something else, you have two options. First, **you can increase the available time and attention you do have.** This may be possible. Exercising regularly and eating well can do this for you. If you are already maxed-out, you can choose the second of the two options, **decrease the amount of time and attention necessary to get the grades you want.** One method of doing this is taking less demanding classes in subject areas where you have little interest, when it makes good sense to do so. There are many other ways.

For example, you're in college. You aspire to be a chemical engineer. You have to take economics and two professors teach it. **Take the class with the fewer requirements.** Expend your energy on activities that interest you. Let's say you're in college, majoring in political science and you have to fulfill certain physical science electives. Make them as simple as possible—free up your time and attention for challenging political science classes. Take a few of your out-of-area requirements pass/no pass. This may sound obvious to some of you, and yet you would be surprised how many students make life hard on themselves by taking difficult, low priority, classes for graded credit.

If there are any readers who gasp at this suggestion, be you parents or teachers—get real! This is simply good common sense. In school you get A's for doing the work. If the work doesn't interest you there is less chance you'll do it, and if you're in a demanding class that usually means lower grades. To get into college and graduate school you need high grades. Nowhere on your transcript is there room for an asterisk indicating that economics with Ms. Jones was tougher than economics with Ms. Roth. **A C is a C and an A is an A.** Your goal is to accumulate as many A's as possible. Furthermore, in the real world you don't get extra credit for making things tougher on yourself. The manager who develops the plan yielding the most return for the least cost gets paid the most. It's the same way in school.

So, when you're putting together your schedule, do so keeping in mind you want a blend of classes that challenge you in the areas that interest you and that are as easy as possible in the areas that don't. If you choose all easy classes, be sure that they will move you towards your long term goal. Also, be sure that you're not setting yourself up to have to take all hard classes in the future. If you choose all hard classes, you run the risk of not having the resources to do well in all of them at the same time. As a result, your grades might suffer. **So do your reconnaissance. Gather your intelligence.** Find out who are the best teachers for each subject, given your goals. In college, I knew students who would meet the professors before they put together their schedules to find out what they were like and what they required. One of my friends was a good test taker and found papers were always much more work for him than tests (this changed drastically in graduate school). If a professor required a paper he usually wouldn't take the class. My friend made it through college having to write only three papers! **You may be surprised at how much time and work you can save yourself by choosing your classes wisely.**

REFERENCES

Samuels, J. S. (1981). Handling procrastination. Unpublished Lecture.

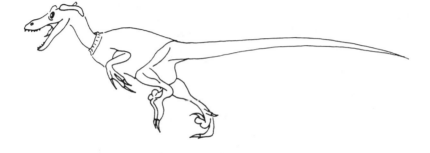

CHAPTER 4

KNOWING WHAT'S GOING TO BE ON THE TEST

In this chapter you will have the opportunity to learn how to determine what is important and what is not when you are studying. We will discuss taking class notes and what to do with them once you've got them. We will also talk about what to do with textbooks. Simply put, if you become competent with the skills in both this chapter and the next, you will begin to know before the fact what will be on your tests. **If you know this, your academic life will be much easier.**

Exercise 4.1 What's important?

Answer the following questions:

What do you study?
How do you know what is important?
What should you pay attention to in class?
How do you know when you're right?

Answer these questions as best you can. Most of you probably never asked yourselves these questions. **If you want to cut down on your workload, have more free time, and still get high grades, you need to know the answers to these questions.**

SO TAKE SOME TIME AND ANSWER THEM.

Did you come up with some answers? Good! Let me guess. Some of you answered "I don't know" and left it at that. Some of you said "Whatever the teacher says is important." Some of you said "It's all important." A few of you probably worked out elaborate rating systems. There are also a few of you who "just know" what to pay attention to and don't know how you know. If you are one of them you are lucky. Please understand that these students are in a very small minority. If you're like most students, you know you should take lots of notes and study them, and do all the assigned readings and study them. While you probably do not do all this, you most likely think you should. I'll tell you, **finding out what's important is incredibly simple, and quite obvious.**

TEST ANALYSIS/POST-TESTING

Exercise 4.2 Test analysis

After you get your tests back, regardless of your grades find the answers to as many of the test questions as you can in your notes. Then find the answers to as many questions as you can in your textbook. Remember to mark down where the answers are located.

This is the most effective way to find out what is important. Not only will you begin to get a sense for what's important information, you will get feedback regarding the quality of your note taking, and you will get a better understanding of how to use your textbooks most efficiently.

If you find about 90% of the answers to the test questions in your notes, your note-taking is very good; 80% is all right. If you find less than 70% of the answers to the questions in your notes, your note-taking is pretty bad. **Those who take excellent notes will often find upwards of 95% of the answers to most of their tests in their notes.** There will be exceptions, though these will be few. Every so often you will have a professor who tests predominantly from the assigned readings and leaves the classes open for discussions. These instructors are rare. In my career as a student I have had only one such teacher. Slightly more common (though also quite rare) is the incompetent teacher, one who really can neither lecture nor teach, and who therefore gives class presentations which are simply drivel. I can recall only two of those in my experience, both in my freshman year of high school. Please remember these are exceptions. If you think you may have had one or two of these instructors each semester, it's more likely that it is you that is the one that is incompetent, not your instructors.

Finding the answers to test questions in your textbooks will help clue you in to what parts of the book your teacher considers important. **You will be able to discover his/her patterns.** Does he take his questions from the graphs and tables? Does she take most of her questions from the definitions? This process can be a real eye-opener. Find out how your teacher uses the textbook and use it the same way. The percentage of answers you will find in your book will vary. It could be as little as 10% and as much as 100%. It depends on the teacher. Some teachers only use textbooks as reference material, a source for their students to pick up the finer points of the subject. Others teach straight from them (some even use their own textbooks). Most, if not all, textbooks come with teachers' copies which include a bank of test questions. Some teachers make up their tests exclusively from this bank. In these cases you'll find 100% of the answers to these tests in the book. A give away will be the ease of finding these answers. They will be in the language of the book.

USING CLASS TIME

TAKING NOTES

Believe it or not, with a few exceptions, **teachers have an order and logic to the material they present to their classes.** Your notes should reflect this order and logic. Therefore, your notes should usually be in the form of an outline. If you can't put the lecture material into an outline form in class, do so as soon as you can after class. If you can't outline—learn how. Find a friend, parent, tutor, teacher, or school counselor that can help you. It may help to review the general format of a presentation (lecture). The format will vary somewhat with the type of class. For example, in a math class the bulk of the instructor's time is spent teaching how to work particular types of problems (e.g., story problems), so few notes are given. In history, the instructor's time is predominantly spent giving information, so many notes are given.

"READING" THE PROFESSOR

The two sources of information in a class are the teacher and the readings. About 95% of the time the teacher is by far the most important. He or she is the one who tells you what's pertinent and what's not. Teachers do this in many ways during their lectures. (For purposes of this section, we are talking about the vast majority of teachers, who <u>are</u> competent). **Therefore, one of the best ways to learn about** what to study is to attend class and pay close attention. **Learn to read your teacher.** Teachers' "reads" can be as obvious as their saying "This will be on the test, so be sure you know it." Or "reads" can be as subtle as their voices getting slightly louder to emphasize a points they think are important. Some typical reads to look for are

> * **The course outline**
> * **What's written on the blackboard**
> * **Repetition - information that's repeated**
> * **Emphasis - "This is important," "OK, listen up"**
> * **An increase in the volume of a teacher's voice.**
> * **An increase in a teacher's movement - she becomes more animated**
> * **An increase in a teacher's intensity**
> * **Any reference to work that a teacher has done**

These are just some of the many possible "reads." Most teachers will give slightly different "reads." When you notice a teacher's "read," pay even more attention. They often indicate what will be on the test.

Exercise 4.3 Your "reading" list

Develop a list of reads for each one of your teachers.

VOCABULARY: THE KEY TO EXCELLING IN MOST SUBJECTS

Were you ever in a science class that seemed like a foreign language class? You know, you couldn't understand a thing, nothing made any sense? Well, that science class was a foreign language class! You see, **every subject has its own language. Master that language, and you will master that class!** It may help you to think of each subject as a foreign language. Doing well in a German class requires that you learn the German equivalents for English words. It's no different for biology, chemistry, sociology, psychology, and many, many other subjects. Like with German, doing well requires that you learn each subject's vocabulary. Sometimes that is all you need to learn! If you take the time at the beginning of each course to familiarize yourself with the vocabulary, you will have a much easier time throughout the term. Whether you're in class or using a textbook, vocabulary is what you need to focus on first.

So what do you do if you simply can't seem to understand the professor's lecture? **Concentrate on developing your fluency with that subject's language.** To do so, simply go to the glossary in your textbook and, taking a sheet of looseleaf paper, write a word in the margin and its definition next to it. Do this for as many words as you need. To learn these words, read over your list, fold your paper at the margin, and test yourself. Keep testing yourself until you know all the definitions.

Make certain you can correctly use these words in sentences, and make sure the sentences you create demonstrate your understanding. For example, take the word "biology," which means "the branch of knowledge that deals with living organisms." Using "biology" in the sentence "I study biology" does not give a clear indication that you know what the word means. You can substitute any number of words for "biology" and still have a sentence that makes sense. A better sentence would be: "My love of animals led me to major in biology." This sentence more clearly indicates that you understand the concept.

Generating sentences in this manner serves two purposes. First, being able to use words correctly indicates that you understand them. If you're having trouble using a word, you probably don't understand it well enough. Second, using new words this way will increases the likelihood that you will remember their meaning and usage in the future—like on tests. **Sometimes this vocabulary practice is the only work you will need to do for a class!**

TEXTBOOKS: TO USE, OR NOT TO USE

Textbooks do have their place and their value. In some classes, such as math, physics, and chemistry, they are absolutely necessary. In other classes they provide valuable sources of reference as well as aid you in understanding the material. Their value, however, is limited to your ability to use them effectively.

Books for math and science classes fall into a special category. They are needed primarily for their practice problems. You should do as many of these problems or procedures as it takes for you to

1) recognize which formulas and procedures apply to which problems and
2) to competently apply these formulas and procedures.

Rule: *Do not, I repeat, <u>do not</u> use highlighters. They are fundamentally evil.*

The bulk of your textbooks require much different handling. Much of how you use them depends on what kind of tests are given in the specific classes. I'll go into greater detail about this in the next chapter. For now, know that for classes in which essay tests predominate, you should outline the chapters in your own words. For classes in which objective tests are the norm (multiple choice, matching, True/False, identification, etc.) use a question-oriented method. The best method I've heard of is taking Post-its® (small sticky pieces of paper) and as you read something important, write a question about it on a Post-it and place it where the answer is in your book. When you go through the book before a test, simply answer all the questions you wrote for yourself. For those questions you miss, go back over them until you answer them correctly.

Exercise 4.4 Outlining

Outline a chapter in your own words.

Exercise 4.5 Post-iting

Post-it a chapter.

* **Remember, before you apply either of these methods (particularly 4.4) run a test analysis to find out what you should pay attention to.**

TOSSING AWAY YOUR TEXTBOOKS

Think about this. For any subject there is a seemingly infinite amount of information. It is a teacher's responsibility to present you with the most important information he can within the time available. If teachers want you to learn as much as you can about the information they consider most important (and most of them do), they will test you on that information. Therefore, almost all of the information they test you on (if they are being responsible) should come from their lectures. And if you take really good notes, this will be reflected in your test analysis. Simply put, **for many of your classes you do not have to use textbooks, provided your note-taking skills are strong.** I know of one student who bought only six textbooks during the last three years of his undergraduate studies.

To test this logic, I ran a little experiment in a pre-med biology class in college. It was a three-quarter class with four tests given each quarter (3 tests and a final). Each test consisted of 50 questions and the finals, 100 questions. Therefore, each quarter we had 250 test questions, and over the three quarters 750 questions. Running a test analysis I found **only 9 questions out of the 750 which had answers that couldn't be found in my notes. That's less than 2 percent!** Now a biology textbook is typically 600 pages long with thousands upon thousands of bits of information. To have read through my text in the hopes of finding those 9 bits of information would have been quite pointless, an amazing waste of time and effort.

Before you start tossing your books away, you'll have to answer three very important questions:

1. **Is your notetaking good enough?**
2. **How much does your teacher rely on the book?**
3. **Do you want to?**

The first question is the most important. Do not answer it until you've done a test analysis. Even if your test analysis reveals that 95% of the answers can be found in your notes, you have to determine how effectively you can use your notes. In some classes textbooks are truly necessary. These include classes such as math, chemistry, physics, or any class where you have to be competent at working problems to succeed. I'll show you how to most effectively use your notes in the next chapter. My suggestion is that no matter how good you think you are at note-taking, withdraw from books slowly. Take a test just using your notes and see how you do. If you ace it—take another. If you get a B on that one, you're not ready yet. Work on your note-taking and other study skills (next chapter). Discontinue using your books only for classes in which you are competent in and in which you feel comfortable doing so.

The second question—how much does your teacher rely on the book?—is not as important as it might seem. Many professor says: "half of the test question will be taken from the lecture and half of the test questions will be taken from the book." In my entire undergraduate career only once did I find this to be true. The great majority of professors cover almost all of the material needed for their tests in their lectures.

A more important question is: "Do I want to do without my textbook?" Some of you like textbooks. Some of you would rather read them than attend class. Some of you use textbooks to clarify the lecture material. Some of you use the lecture material to point out what you need to focus on in your books. If you have a system that works for you—great! Keep it up! And if you want to try something different, it is my belief that many of you can get high grades (while saving time and money) without textbooks in many of your classes.

OTHER READINGS

Besides textbooks, other reading material you will almost certainly encounter in either high school or college will include the study of literature and research.

THE STUDY OF LITERATURE

Literature, of course, includes novels, short stories, plays, and poetry. When you read this kind of material keep your goal in mind. **Know what you are reading for.** You very rarely have to read the entire book. Of course, if you want to, by all means do so. If you're supposed to write a paper based upon a particular format, read your book keeping that format at hand. Look for the specific information you need to fill out the format. Most often you will be asked to analyze a work. When reading for this type of assignment, look for motifs that are repeated, and be sensitive to symbolism in order to discover prominent themes. **If you're reading a book in order to discuss it in class, become very familiar with a few parts so you can intelligently contribute to the class discussion.**

With this type of reading there are many methods to make efficient use of your time. Probably the most popular is not reading a book at all. It is very difficult to get an A in a literature class with this approach, although it has been known to happen. Probably the second most popular short cut is using Cliff Notes (or other such outlines) when available in lieu of reading an actual novel, play, etc. This works. I've also heard of students watching movies based on books instead of reading them. If you choose this method, hope that the movie is a close adaptation of the book. It's a dead give-away that you haven't read a book when you discuss a character that is not in the novel on a test.

One of the best methods I know to make better use of your time in your lit classes is to prioritize the reading lists. At the top of your list, of course, will be **the books that are most important to your instructor. Make sure you know which they are.** You can easily tell how important a work is by the amount of time your instructor spends on it—the more time, the more important. You can skip a couple of books if you know they are low priority. It's rare that you will have to discuss all the works on a final—you usually get a choice.

Another good method to make better use of your time in classes that require a lot of this type of reading is working in small groups (groups of 3 or 4). Within the group, divide the reading up equally, making each member responsible for a comprehensive outline of the readings the group assigns them. This is a very common practice in law school, where the amount of reading is legendary. **Be sure, if you choose this approach, to select responsible and intelligent group members.** Their outlines are all you will have to work with for two-thirds to three-quarters of the material.

RESEARCH

In many respects reading research material is similar to textbook reading and the same basic procedures apply. The main difference is in the format of the writing. In textbooks the information is organized as follows:

> A. Information (Theory)
>   1. Explanation (including defining terms)
>   2. Examples
> B. Information (Theory)
>   1. Explanation (including defining terms)
>   2. Examples

If you understand the theory being introduced, you need not pay attention to the explanations and the examples. If you do not fully understand the theory, read as much of the explanation as you need. If, after reading the explanations, you still do not fully understand the theory, pay attention to the examples.

The format of scientific research is generally as follows:

A. Introduction
   1. History
   2. Hypothesis
B. Experiment
C. Results
D. Conclusion

In most cases you need to know who did the research, the hypothesis, a brief overview of the experiment, a statement of the results (i.e., was the hypothesis supported or not), and what the researcher(s) concluded. This can usually all be put on one side of a 3 x 5 index card (flashcard). If you're writing a paper, you need to know if the report supports or undermines your own hypothesis. Do you have to read research material for a test? Run a test analysis and find out. Usually the answer will be no.

Exercise 4.6 Summarizing research articles

Put the important points of a research article on a single index card.

NOTE TO TEACHERS:

While most of us understand the relationship between student and teacher to be a cooperative one, there are a few of you who believe the relationship to be a competitive one. Your goal when you test your students is to stump them rather than to test their knowledge of critical concepts and issues. Your goal when you teach them is to make them do all the work, rather than present them with new viewpoints and opportunities to learn. To you, reading twenty pages is more important than understanding them. It is you few teachers who will, after having read this chapter, view this as an "us against them" game. You will believe I am simply teaching students to "Psych out the test" or "Psych out the teacher" and so you will attempt to make your tests "unpsychable," and in the process **you will have completely missed the point.**

Today, our society is information-oriented. So much new information is becoming available daily that keeping up with it all is impossible. **To succeed in this society, our students are going to need to be able to know what information is important and what is not.** Our school system provides our students with an excellent laboratory to develop this skill. The classroom in this respect models the real world quite well. Between classes, lectures, and reading assignments, our students are presented with a huge body of information—only a portion of which is important. It is their job to determine what is and is not important. If they do a good job they do well in their classes.

This is what this chapter is really about. Asking them to do all the work is valuable. **It is also valuable for them to select which parts of the work they do. The very best students have this skill down to a science,** whether or not they can articulate it. We need to help more of our students become similarly competent. Exercises like those in this chapter are designed to meet this need.

CHAPTER 5

STUDYING:

WHAT WORKS, AND WHY

All right, people! This is the chapter that counts! You are about to learn the best ways to study! I will tell you right from the start, most of you are doing it wrong. If you are parents or teachers, then most of you did it wrong. If you are successful now or have been in the past you were most likely successful in spite of the way you studied, not because of it. READY? Good. Here is the first exercise:

Exercise 5.1 How will you study?

You have three tests coming up: history, biology and algebra. How will you study for them? (If it makes any difference, the history test is mostly essay and the biology test is multiple choice).

OK! Let's see. If you're a typical student you said you would prepare for the algebra test by going over your notes and practicing problems in the book. For both the history and biology tests you would reread your notes over and over again, and you would go over the book, paying particular attention to the parts you highlighted. Also, if you're like most students, you will cram for these tests the night before and/or the day of the test. This is what most students do. This will work for those with the ability to remember all that they've read after one or two readings. For the rest of us it's really ineffective. How many of you use or have used highlighters (you know, the colored, florescent markers) on your notes & books? Personally I find this quite entertaining and somewhat silly. You will too, by the time we are finished.

Highlighting is perhaps the silliest of all study techniques. At best it is slightly better than just reading. At worst it seriously gets in the way of preparing for a test. For those of you not yet in college and perhaps not exposed to this mythological ritual, highlighting involves taking a brightly colored transparent marker and coloring the parts of your notes and/or textbook that you feel are important. In the first part of this chapter we will explore why highlighting and other typical approaches to studying are so inefficient and ineffective as we look at how our memory works.

THE MEMORY SYSTEM —

Why what works, works.
Why what doesn't work, doesn't work.

This section is going to be theoretical and somewhat technical. I urge the reader to take the time to understand this material, as this understanding is critical if you are going to flourish as STUDENTS and develop your own, personalized methods of learning.

There are a number of different models of the memory system. Some break up the system into parts (e.g., short-term and long-term memory). Others break it down according to the levels at which we process information (e.g., visual, acoustic, semantic). For this discussion it doesn't matter which way you look at the system. The only issues that really matter are simply

* **Encoding—** putting information in, and
* **Retrieving—** getting information out.

How do we get stuff (information) into our memory (encoding), in such a way as to make it easy to get that stuff back out again (retrieval)? If we expect to need to know the names of all the planets in our solar system for a test, what method of studying them (encoding) gives us the best chance of knowing (retrieving) them when we are tested?

If you can retrieve the information you want, it was encoded adequately; if you can't, it was not encoded adequately.

Five factors that affect our chances of retrieving (remembering) information are

1. **the type of encoding activity**
2. **retrieval practice**
3. **spacing**
4. **the interaction between retrieval and spacing**
5. **the match between study and test**

ACTIVE AND PASSIVE ENCODING   (Craik, 1981)

Encoding comes in two general forms: active and passive. Passive encoding is encoding (putting in) the information in the same form in which it is presented. Active encoding is encoding the information in a different form from which it was presented. For example, when you read a paragraph you are passively encoding it. When you take the same paragraph and rewrite it in your own words, you are actively encoding it.

PRINCIPLE #1

a) **Active encoding is in almost every case better than passive encoding.**
b) **For a study technique to work efficiently it has to involve active encoding.**

c) The material should be encoded in such a
way that retrieval practice should come as
close as possible to simulating the test.

Therefore when you study it is **important that you change
the form of the information in some way.** Highlighting is
passive encoding, you are not changing the form of the
information. Any study method that requires a change in the
form of the information by the student (e.g., outlining chapters,
making up Post-it questions) will be more effective than those
that don't.

THE RETRIEVAL PRACTICE EFFECT (Bjork, 1975, 1979)

The retrieval practice effect is simply that **the more often you
retrieve (remember) a piece of information correctly, the
greater the chances are that you'll remember it at some later
date.** In essence, the act of remembering is an act of encoding.
It works like this: Let's say I give you a list of the planets in our
solar system (Mercury, Venus, Earth, Mars, Jupiter, Saturn,
Uranus, Neptune, and Pluto) and I tell you that you can learn
them in one of two ways. One (most common), you can read
over them or two, you can simply try to recall (retrieve) them.
If you do the latter and try to recall them, provided you recall
them accurately, you will remember them much better than if
you chose the former method and simply read over them. This
is critical to understand.

PRINCIPLE #2

Recalling   information   correctly   greatly
increases   your   chances   of   recalling   that
information correctly at a later date.

STUDENTS: Therefore, for a study technique to be most effective **it must provide you with an opportunity to retrieve the pertinent information.** In this way retrieving is a type of active encoding. You are changing the form of the information simply by asking for it.

If a study technique does not provide this opportunity (as the common ones do not—e.g., reading over notes or highlighted   material again and again), your chances of remembering the information will be severely diminished.

TEACHERS: This   principle   suggests   that   the   more opportunities   you   provide   for   your   students   to   recall information, the greater the chances are that they will remember it.

THE SPACING EFFECT (Landauer and Bjork, 1979)

The spacing effect concerns the spacing with which information is repeatedly presented. Psychologists have found that up to a point the greater the distance between two presentations of the same information, the greater the likelihood that information will be recalled correctly.   For example, if I am going to tell you a phone number three times, the chances of you recalling it are greater if I tell it to you once an hour for 3 hours than if I tell it to you once a minute for 3 minutes. Your chances are even greater if I tell it to you once a day for 3 days. At some distance we will reach the point of diminishing returns.

PRINCIPLE #3

As the distance between presentations of the same   information   increase   so   does   the

probability that that information will be recalled correctly (up to a point).

  STUDENTS: Therefore, a study technique that provides you the opportunity to space out the times that you go over the same material is more efficient than one that requires you repeat the same information at fairly short intervals. This explains why cramming for tests is somewhat effective for the short term and almost completely ineffective for the long term.

  TEACHERS: Applying this principle increases the chances that your students will learn the material you judge to be most important. Doing so requires that you repeat such material at well spaced intervals.

EXPANDED RETRIEVAL PRACTICE
(Murray and Bjork, 1986)

  Expanded retrieval practice is the most efficient and effective method for long-term recall. The principle of expanded retrieval practice states that as the distance between study (encoding) and testing (retrieving) increases, two things happen:

1. the chances of correct recall decrease
2. however, if the information is recalled correctly, the chances that that information will be recalled correctly at a much later date will greatly increase.

So if I give you a telephone number at 1:00 p.m. and ask you to recall that number at 1:01 p.m., your chances of being right are greater than if I ask you to recall the number at 3:00 p.m. However, if you recalled it correctly at 3:00 p.m., your chances of recalling it correctly at 7:00 p.m. are far greater than if you only recalled it correctly at 1:01 p.m.

PRINCIPLE #4

a) The closer a recall attempt is to the time of study, the greater the chances are that you will recall the information accurately.

b) Given a successful recall attempt, the farther that attempt is from the time of study, the greater the chances are that a second recall attempt at an even greater distance will be successful.

To apply this principle to studying, you need to space your retrieval practice in such a way as to take best advantage of the spacing effect. For example:

```
Study  Test      Test       Test                Test     Actual
       Yourself  Yourself   Yourself            Yourself  Test
            ---------------------- time ---------------------->
```

MATCHING STUDY TO TEST

This last principle is really obvious. It involves the similarity between how you study and how you will be tested.

PRINCIPLE #5

The more closely your study methods match the type of test you are to take, the more likely you are to retrieve (remember) the appropriate information.

Remember our discussion on encoding? If you're studying for a short-answer test, change the form of the information in such a way as to require yourself to answer questions about specific bits of information (e.g., by using flashcards or Post-its). If you're studying for an essay test, change the form of the information in such a way as to require yourself to reorganize, or reorder the information (e.g., outlining).

To summarize what we have discussed, for a study technique to be efficient and effective, it has to demand that you actively change the information in some meaningful way, preferably in a way that makes it easy to practice retrieving it. The technique should also allow for the practice of expanded retrieval. Lastly, the encoding and subsequent retrieval practice should come as close as possible to mimicking actual test conditions.

MNEMONICS

Before we move on to discuss specific study techniques and their application, I want to say a few words about mnemonics. **Mnemonics are simply aids to memory.** They come in many shapes and sizes, from limited, one-shot aids (such as "Every Good Boy Does Fine" to help us remember the lines on a musical staff), to more involved and more adaptable link and peg systems. The generation and application of these tools are seemingly unlimited. I will not go into detail here concerning these mnemonics tools. Rather, given our previous discussion, I want to mention the logic behind why they work and why they are so valuable. They work simply because they demand highly active encoding. To successfully use these tools you (the student) have to become very involved in the process. It is this involvement that is the cornerstone of the workability of mnemonic devices.

NOTE TO TEACHERS:

Mnemonics also have value above and beyond their usefulness as aids to memory that is sometimes overlooked by those who are adept with such tools. The successful use of mnemonics seem to have an amazingly positive effect on a student's self-image. Imagine a student who thinks poorly of himself discovering he is able to remember a list of 20 or 30 items in and out of order! **I have seen such a demonstration change lives. Because of this I strongly recommend that teachers become competent with basic mnemonic techniques and provide their students with an experience that will often help them throughout their lives.** The best book that I know of on this subject is <u>The Memory Book</u> by Harry Lorayne and Jerry Lucas. It can be found in most bookstores and only costs four or five dollars. It's a great investment.

THE RIGHT TOOL FOR THE RIGHT JOB

Harken back to the exercise at the beginning of this chapter. Different types of classes typically use different types of tests, which call for different preparations. **In order to succeed you need to understand these differences and have an arsenal of tools you can use to prepare for each variation.** In this next section we will discuss the various types of classes you will encounter during your schooling. These are classified by the kinds of tests you will find in them. There are basically three kinds of classes:

1. Problem-oriented classes
2. Performance-oriented classes
3. Information-oriented classes

PROBLEM-ORIENTED CLASSES

Problem-oriented classes are **classes in which tests require you to solve problems.** The best examples of problem-oriented classes are math classes. Other classes that usually fall into this category are most physic and chemistry classes, as well as many engineering classes. This is particularly true in college. **Your success in these classes is predicated on your ability to work problems,** a sort of grading by the numbers. If you know the right formulas for the problems, where all the numbers belong, and which numbers are added, subtracted, multiplied, and divided, you will do well.

There are a few students who are gifted in these subjects. These are the students who actually understand the theories underlying the formulas. They really know what quantum mechanics is all about. They could probably generate a formula from their knowledge of an underlying theory. Most of us (myself included) are not one of these gifted few. Happily, you don't need to be in order to succeed. You really need to understand very little. **You simply have to know what formula applies to what circumstance, and how to apply it.** This is solely a matter of mechanics.

Typically, tests in these classes are 80% problem-solving and 20% short-answer involving mostly vocabulary and theory. Preparing for these tests is pretty straight forward:

1. Memorize all the formulae necessary
2. Work the problems at the end of each chapter in your textbook until you master the mechanics
3. Study your vocabulary and understand the main concepts

Make sure you know 1 and 2 before you work on 3. By the way, it is usually **only in problem-oriented classes that homework is almost always useful.** Do it with an eye towards the tests. Do extra problems if you have to to become mechanically proficient at the problem-working skills. Remember, if you need help—get it! And get it before the test!

PERFORMANCE-ORIENTED CLASSES

As in problem-oriented classes in which your grades are mostly based on your ability to solve problems, not your accumulated knowledge, your grades in performance-oriented classes are based primarily on what you can do, not what you know. These are basically skill classes. A writing class is an example of a performance-oriented class. Other examples include music performance classes, studio art classes, drama classes, and P.E. classes. In these classes there often are not any tests at all. **Your grade in these classes is based primarily on your performance.** In writing classes what you write about is not nearly as important as how you write about it. Creativity is often rewarded. Preparing for performance-oriented classes involves practicing correctly. Remember "Practice does not make perfect. Perfect practice makes perfect." Remember the levels of learning—practice a skill until you in fact are competent at it. Most students encounter fewer of these classes than either the problem- or information-oriented types. In fact, unless you major in writing, music, art, or some such discipline you may not see more than four or five of these classes during your stay in college.

INFORMATION-ORIENTED CLASSES

Information-oriented classes are the type of classes the majority of students most often encounter. In these classes **your grade is based almost entirely on your ability to recall bits of information.** The more you can recall, the higher your grade, and the better organized your information is the easier it will be to recall. All classes in the life sciences and social sciences are information-oriented, as well as in most business classes and some classes in the humanities. Biology, geology, psychology, anthropology, history, sociology, social studies, physiology, kinesiology, marketing, economics, and many more subject areas fall under this classification. It is in these classes that your ability to determine what is important, organize it, encode it, and retrieve it is at a premium.

In these classes there are generally two types of tests: objective tests and essay tests. Objective tests may include multiple-choice questions, true/false questions, identification questions, fill-in-the-blank questions, and/or matching questions.

Essay tests come in two general varieties: 100% essay and 80% essay. The 100% variety are tests that are solely essay and are typically found in literature classes. The 80% variety are tests in which essays will be worth 80% of the grade; the remaining 20% will be in the form of identification questions in which you are given a name or concept and have to describe it in 3 or 4 sentences. This type of test is most often found in history classes. You should note that the typical essay test will usually require that you write an essay on one or two out of three or four subject options. Often these topics are discrete; that is, they have little to do with one another. Sometimes they are continuous; that is, they demand that you integrate all the material covered throughout the testing period. Continuous essays are usually the more challenging of the two, though they are somewhat more rare.

Objective tests and essay tests require different preparations. **Generally speaking, for objective tests you should use a study method that involves some kind of question/answer work on your part. For essay tests you should use a study method that allows for overall reorganization of the material.**

A word about studying languages. The best advice I have ever heard for students beginning to study a foreign language—**master three verbs: to be, to do, to have.** These are the three most commonly used verbs (by far) in all human language. Master these and you'll have gone a long way towards being able to speak the language. I suspect almost all language teachers know this. It's just that so few of them actually make it clear to their students.

Problem-, performance-, and information-oriented classes are the three basic types of classes you will encounter. There are, of course, variations on these themes; for instance, some physics tests will be 50% problems and 50% multiple-choice questions, and in days past chemistry tests were 100% essay tests. Regardless, **the most important thing to remember about this section is that for each class you take you must keep in mind the method of evaluation.**

Exercise 5.2 What kinds of classes are you taking?

Identify the types of all the classes you are currently taking and will be taking in the foreseeable future.

For example:

Class	Test	Type
Biology	Multiple Choice	Info
History	80% Essay/20% Identification	Info
Algebra	90% Problem/10% Matching	Problem

STUDY TECHNIQUES THAT WORK... AND WHY

Now it's time for specifics. In this section we will look at five study techniques that work attending to why they work and how best to apply them. These five techniques are

1. Questioning
2. Reorganizing (outlining)
3. Rote Practices
4. Teaching
5. Group Study

Be advised that some of these approaches will be new to you. In this case they will take more work than you are used to while you master them. Your old ways will likely seem easier to you. This is because you are more familiar with them. Rest assured that if you put in the time to become proficient with

these new techniques you will be well rewarded. Be patient.
Be diligent. Are you READY? Good. Let's get going.

QUESTIONING TECHNIQUES: FLASHCARDING

Questioning techniques include any study method that has
you formulate questions and answer them. The Post-it
method discussed in the previous chapter is a good example of
such a technique. One of the best questioning techiques is
"Flashcarding." Using flashcards is by far the most effective
technique for preparing for objective tests. It involves **deriving
questions and answers from the material you are studying** by
creating flashcards with a question on one side and its answer
on the other. I cannot over-emphasize the benefits you will
gain by flashcarding or using some similar technique.
Flashcarding has advantages both as a study tool and a
training tool. As a study tool, flashcarding demands that you
actively involve yourself in encoding (i.e., in order to turn
lecture material into questions and answers you have to
change the form of the material).   Once information is
flashcarded, it is then easy to apply expanded retrieval practice,
or if you're not so inclined, to simply take advantage of the
retrieval practice effect. In simple English, this means you get
many chances to test yourself before a test. As a training tool,
flashcarding has even greater advantages.   You find out
immediately how well you know the material. If you can form
questions that are similar to those that will appear on the test,
you know the material well; if not, you don't know it as well as
you probably need to. Next, **flashcarding provides you with
an exercise to develop your ability to predict what will be on
the test.** Flashcarding can also provide you with a guide for
improved notetaking. As far as I'm concerned, flashcarding is
the single most effective and beneficial tool there is in a
student's arsenal.

HOW TO MAKE FLASHCARDS

Get a pack of 3 x 5 index cards and as soon as possible after class sit down and put the day's notes on flashcards. Make up a question on one side and put the answer on the other. If you take notes in outline form this will be easy. If you do not take notes in outline form—learn to. Let's take this section of the chapter up to this point as an example:

Card 1, Side 1

What are the five study techniques that work?
card 1

Card 1, Side 2

1. Questioning	4. Teaching
2. Outlining/Reorganizing	5. Group Study
3. Rote practice	

Card 2, Side 1

1. Questioning (What is it?)
2 Which is the most effective technique?
card 2

Card 2, Side 2

1. Taking material and deriving questions and answers from it
2. Flashcarding

Card 3, Side 1

> What are the three advantages of flashcarding as a study tool?
>
>   card 3

Card 3, Side 2

> 1. It's active encoding
> 2. It allows for easy expanded retrieval practice
> 3. It takes advantage of the retrieval/practice effect

Card 4, Side 1

> What are the three advantages of flashcarding as a training tool?
>
>   card 4

Card 4, Side 2

> 1. It helps you find out how well you know the material
> 2. It helps you develop your ability to predict test questions
> 3. Its a guide to improve your note taking

Remember to number your cards. This will be necessary when you study from them. There is no strict form for flashcarding. As your skill improves you will develop your own symbols, codes, and shorthand. I know this seems like a lot of extra work, and at first it is. Trust me, once you get proficient at it, flashcarding your notes goes pretty quickly. If **you master the technique you will often not have to take any notes at all.** You will be able to sit in many of your classes with only your 3 x 5 index cards and flashcard as your professor lectures.

One last word about flashcarding. Using flashcards someone else has made isn't nearly as effective as making your own. Why? Because you lose the enormous advantage of active encoding. When you use another student's flashcards you only passively encode the material. I do not recommend this. Take the time and develop your own ability to flashcard. **Only when you get good at it will you understand what a mind-blowing tool flashcarding really is.**

Making up questions on Post-its from material in textbooks is another questioning technique that works. You can also flashcard chapters of textbooks. Both methods work just fine. If you're going to use textbooks and attend classes, I strongly advise that you **Post-it or flashcard only those portions of the book that are not covered (or that are not covered adequately enough for you), in class.** I'm sure there are other questioning techniques. If you know of any and they work for you, use them. If you are so inclined, create your own. It can be a wonderful learning experience.

HOW TO USE YOUR FLASHCARDS

Once you have your notes flashcarded, set aside your notes (you may never have to look at them again). **When it's time to prepare for a test, just use your cards.** Let's say you have 60 cards for a test you are about to take. Take the first 20 and read through them once (twice if you think you need to). Now test yourself. Sort out those questions that you get wrong and test yourself on those until you get them correct. When you answer a question correctly, put it back with the others. Repeat this routine with the next 20 cards, then the next. Finally go through all 60 cards. When you can go through them all correctly you're ready for the test. Under optimal circumstances you would do this about a week before the test, then again about four days before the test, then again the night before. However, this routine works just fine if you use it only the day before your test, particularly if it's the only time you will be tested on the material. Use your own judgment. **Remember, do what is necessary to accomplish the goal.**

WHEN TO USE YOUR FLASHCARDS

As I stated before, flashcarding is the method of choice for all objective tests. There is simply no comparable substitute. Flashcarding is also useful for problem-oriented classes such as physics and chemistry—classes where you need to have many formulas memorized. In these classes simply flashcard the formulas and the definitions of terms you are presented with. Remember, though, spend most of your study time working problems when you prepare for these classes. I personally have found flashcards to be of limited use for essay tests, though your experience may be different. If you can make them work—go for it!

Exercise 5.3 Flashcarding

Flashcard the lecture notes of one or more of your information-oriented classes in which you will have objective tests.

One last thought on flashcards. If you're in college and you think you may be interested in graduate school—save your cards. They will be invaluable when you prepare for your entrance exams, most of which are objective tests covering all of the material in your major area of focus.

REORGANIZING TECHNIQUES — OUTLINING

Outlining and other approaches that have you restructure information are very effective study techniques for essay tests. **Essay tests usually ask you to order information around one or two key concepts. When you study for these tests, you should do the same.** For example, if you're studying early American history, you can order events around battles, around statesmen, or around some changing aspect of colonial life— commerce, perhaps. It will be extremely helpful to create some theory or viewpoint about these topics from which you can use events to argue, for or against, that theory or viewpoint. While such reorganizing may take a fair amount of time at first, **it too will come faster with practice.** Please note that for many classes outlining itself will provide a sufficient enough reordering for you to recall pertinent details. If you are new to this technique, start with outlining.

Once you have the necessary information reorganized and re-outlined (actively encoded), **start coming up with practice essay questions, and write up some outlines to answer them** without using your notes (retrieval practice). **With practice, your questions will start to resemble the actual test questions.** You will also learn to listen for possible test questions when you're in class.

Exercise 5.4 Reorganizing

Reorder and/or outline the material necessary for your next essay test.

ROTE PRACTICE

Rote practice involves doing a task over and over again until you are competent. Rote practice is usually what it takes to become mechanically proficient at solving problems in most math, physics, and chemistry classes

TEACHING

An old saying goes, "the best way to learn something is to teach it." **If you can teach a subject, you really know it.** If you think you really know a subject, try to teach it and find out. Almost everyone who has ever taught anything to anyone has reported that they learned more through the experience than their students. Teaching is a real education. Teaching demands that you have the material highly organized and integrated. To get the material to this state requires active encoding. To teach it requires retrieval practice. That's why this is such a good learning technique. It is an especially good technique when the material is heavily theoretical and the test you are preparing for is an essay type test. Even when the test is objective, if you don't quite grasp the material, sit someone down and teach it to them. Teach your mom, dad, brother, sister, friends, relatives—anyone that would be willing to help you.

When you're teaching someone, make sure they understand. Ask them questions to make sure you got your point across. Otherwise, they will almost always say they understand when they don't, just to please you or shut you up. In those cases, you have not taught them anything. Teaching to learn can be a lot of work and it's really worth it. **The confidence you will get from teaching is immeasurable.** For me, it is one of the most fun ways to learn. If you've never tried it, try it and see what happens.

Exercise 5.5 Teaching

Pick a concept and teach it to someone.

GROUP STUDY

If you do it right, group study can be a great experience. A group is defined as more than one individual. I got through chemistry in college with A's in my 2nd & 3rd quarters only because I worked with a partner. The greatest advantage to working with a group is that **you will have the opportunity to verbally restructure the material (active encoding) and teach it to your partners (retrieval practice).**

If a group is going to be effective it must allow for both of these to occur. Also, **for a group to work the members must become group-, not self-oriented.** This means you do what is best for the group. **Winning is defined as "everyone accomplishing their goals."** The group members all need to be coming from this viewpoint for the best results. In addition, all the members must be willing and able to share the responsibility and to be focused. Groups are notorious for wasting time. Groups are also notorious for unfair contributions. You know, one member does most of the work and the others slack off. Another common occurrence is the dominance of a single member, usually the one most competent with the material. If this person is a good teacher and provides the others with many opportunities to restructure the material and teach it, the group can work. However, if this person is not a good teacher and simply does all the talking while the other members remain passive, the group will be for the most part ineffective.

In my experience I have rarely seen groups work. However, **when they do work, they usually have only 2 or 3 members who are unusually supportive of each other.** When everything is right and a group clicks, it can be one of the best educational experiences you can have. My suggestion is to feel free to try it, and rely on your own resources until the group provides you with evidence you can count on the group's resources.

The above are some basic study tools that work. They are not the only techniques possible. As you proceed through your schooling, you will probably have opportunities to create your own study tools. When you are doing so, remember: for a technique to be effective, **the encoding needs to be active, and retrieval practice must be built into the system.** Keeping these two guides in mind will not only allow you to develop your own effective techniques, they will allow you to better evaluate the many other techniques you encounter.

CREATIVE STUDY STRATEGIES:

PLOTTING AND SCHEMING

The previous section dealt with the specifics of studying. This section focuses on designing your overall study strategies—your approaches to your classes. **When designing your strategies, be creative. Look for speed and effectiveness. Look for shortcuts!** What is the simplest and most effective way to get an A (or whatever grade you want)? If you haven't given this question a lot of consideration before, it's time you do. How you prepare for a test, what tools you use, how much time you spend, and what you actually work on is up to you. **The less work you make for yourself the more time you have to play.**

Many of your classes will be standard, as we have discussed. The study strategies for these will be pretty straightforward. However, you all will encounter your share of non-standard professors with non-standard approaches. I've encountered my share and I know there are others out there. **The best tool you have is your ability to focus on your goal and ascertain the best way to go after it.**

Exercise 5.6 Creative strategies

The following are some examples of non-standard classes. Write down how you would prepare for these classes.

1. Business: Marketing

You are told at the beginning of the class that your grade will based on ten quizzes and a paper. (All questions will require a two- or three-sentence answer.) Each quiz will cover the material in one of the ten chapters in the textbook. You can take as many quizzes at a time as you want (all the first week, all the last week, any combination), and you have to get a perfect score on each quiz to pass. If you do not pass a quiz, you can take it again. A list of 17 questions per chapter will be given to you the first day of class. Quizzes will consist of 5 of these questions selected by the professor. How would you prepare?

2. Psychology: Behavior Modification

Go at your own pace.   The textbook will consist of 32 chapters with 3 quizzes at the end of each one. (All questions will be "fill-in-the-blank") You will be instructed to work in pairs, read the chapter, ask each other questions about each chapter until you both agree you understand it, and initial a form indicating that both of you read and checked out the chapter. You may do this in or out of class. After you and your partner complete a chapter you will take one of the three quizzes at the end of the chapter (to be decided by the professor). How would you prepare?

3. 20th Century American History

Straightforward. Three essay tests. On each test you will have a choice of one of three essays plus five identification questions. How would you prepare?

CREATIVE APPROACHES TO THESE CLASSES

1. Business: Marketing

Take each question, find the answer in the chapter, and make a flashcard. Do this for two chapters per week. Once you have these down, take an educated guess on the questions the professor will ask on a third chapter (if the prof assigned all even-numbered questions for the chapter last week, prepare the odd-numbered questions.   Try about about seven questions.) Each week take three quizzes. You should pass the two you prepared all the questions for, and once in a while you will luck out and pass the third (having selected the right questions to prepare for). If you don't pass the third quiz you can always take it again, and more than one-third of the work is already done. You could finish all the quizzes in about four weeks, take a week to do the paper, and be finished with the class half way through the quarter.

2. Psychology: Behavior Modification

This is also a "go at your own pace" course, remember? Team up with a friend, who, like yourself, is interested in completing the class as quickly as possible. Each of you go to your own home and flashcard all the questions and answers for each of the three quizzes, for the first five or six chapters. One hour before class check each other's answers, then go to class and take the first five or six quizzes. Prepare five or six quizzes for each of the next five classes. You both could be done in six class days! Needless to say you don't need to read the chapters or check each other out. You do, however, need to sign the sheets saying that you have.

3. 20th-Century American History

This was somewhat of a trick question. You will need one test to discover that the professor gives discrete essay tests, that is, each essay question is on a different topic (e.g., one essay on World War I, one essay on the Red Scare, and a third on the Great Depression). For the remaining two tests you will need to study only one of the major topics to be covered by the test for which you are preparing (e.g., World War II for test 2, and the Cold War for test 3), along with some vocabulary (for the identification questions). To prepare for these tests you could outline the information for these topics, write practice essay questions, and outline your answers. Not only could you significantly reduce your study time (for you would need to prepare only one-third of the material), if you were adventurous, you could probably get by attending only two weeks of classes (one for each of the major topics you need to prepare for), and skip the rest.

While you may never have classes that make the demands the   above classes make, and while you may not be adventurous enough to approach a history class in the manner suggested, **you need to be prepared to approach each of your classes differently.** If you are so prepared, you will often be able to save yourself much time and work. **Be creative. Look for shortcuts. Learn what really is necessary to get what you want and use the best tool to get the job done. This is the essence of being a** *STUDENT.*

Exercise 5.7 Plotting and scheming

Determine how you will approach each of your current classes.

REFERENCES

Bjork, R. A. (1975). Retrieval as a memory modifier. In R.
Solso (Ed.), Information processing and cognition: *The*
Loyola Symposium. Hillsdale, NJ: Lawerence Erlbaum
Associates.

Bjork, R. A. (1979). Retrieval Practice. Paper presented at the
conference for developmental and experimental approaches
to human memory. Ann Arbor, MI.

Craik, F. I. M. (1981). Encoding and retrieval effects in human
memory: A partial review. In A. D. Baddely & J. Long (Eds.),
Attention and performance ix. Hillsdale, NJ: Erlbaum.

Landauer, T. K. & Bjork, R. A. (1979). Optimal rehersal patterns
and name learning. In M. M. Greenburg, P. E. Morris, & R. N.
Sykes (Eds.), *Practical aspects of memory*. London: Academic
Press.

Murray, J. T. & Bjork, R. A. (1986). Toward a retrieval practice
interpretation of spacing effects. Unpublished Manuscript.

CHAPTER 6

TEST - TAKING MASTERY

Taking tests can be fun! Tests can be a great time! They are events to be thoroughly enjoyed! I'll bet most of you have never quite looked at tests in this light before. That's OK! You can start now.   Tests are particularly fun when you are confident you know the material. You know—when you are properly prepared and you know it. In fact, tests can also be great when you are confident you don't know the material. You know—when you aren't properly prepared and you know it. In this chapter we are going to talk about taking tests: what to do before tests, during tests, and after tests. **Keep in mind that the grace and style with which you go through an event is as important as the outcome of that event.**

BEFORE THE TEST

If you've taken good notes, studied your flashcards, prepared your outlines, and practiced working your problems until you are competent, you are as ready as you can be—**relax.** If you've done only part of your work, and you're not as prepared as you could be—**relax.** If you have not done any of your work, and you are not prepared at all—**relax.**   Relax, because it is one of the most constructive things you can do. So, in the words of Bobby McFerrin, "Don't worry. Be happy."

The only time this advice may not apply is when you decide to cram right before a test. If this is your chosen study method, follow the above advice at least until you begin cramming.   I can't count all the students I have encountered who know they won't do any real studying until the night before a test and still spend the previous two nights worrying about it. If you know you're not going to really work until the night before the test, enjoy yourself before then.   **If you are planning to worry,**

you'd be better off studying. If you have difficulty with doing work before you think you have to, refer back to Chapter 3 and practice the Procrastination Killer.

This exception aside, many of the best students actually complete their preparation for a test a day or so in advance, especially for big tests. What I suggest is that you get all your preparation done by about 6 or 7 p.m. the night before a test. **Be confident of what you know.** It is always better to go into a test focusing on what you know than on what you don't know. Once you're done studying, relax. Go to a movie. Hang out with your boyfriend or girlfriend. Watch T.V. Work on a hobby. Take a walk. Do whatever you enjoy doing that is relaxing. (Whatever else you do, stay straight.) Before you go to bed, prepare all the things you will need for the test (pencils, pocket calculator, books, etc.). Then **get a good night's rest.** This relaxing and resting time will give your mind time to integrate the information. Get up. Eat a good breakfast. Do what you normally do, then go take the test.

DURING THE TEST

The test actually begins about 10-30 minutes before it is handed to you. You will do better if you take this viewpoint. During this time, prepare yourself, your mind, and your body for the test. If you already have a method to prepare yourself that works, use it. If not, you can use the following method.

Exercise 6.1 Preparing yourself, your mind, and your body for a test.

1. Begin breathing slowly and deeply from your diaphragm (i.e., your midsection). You'll want to breathe about 8-12 times per minute. (less is fine also)

2. Center yourself. Bring all your attention to the here and now. Focus on your breathing—only on your breathing. Do this for a few minutes.

3. While still keeping your breathing nice and steady, begin to fill up your mind with the information you'll need for the text. Pay attention to those things that you know. Feel all that information flow into your awareness. Get a sense that whatever you need will be available.

4. Know that you are as ready you can be.

5. Once you get the test, stay focused on it until you are finished.

OBJECTIVE TESTS

If you're taking an objective test, start at the beginning, read each question carefully, then answer it. If you're unsure of the answer or what the question is asking, make a note and go on to the next question. With multiple-choice questions, there are typically two decent answers, and one of those is the best one. If you can narrow a question down to these two answers, pick the best one, and move on. If you can't narrow down the choices, make a note, and move on. **If you are well prepared, most answers to multiple choice tests are fairly obvious.** When you've gone through the test once, go back and do your best on the questions you skipped, then check all your answers. Only change answers if you are certain your original answer was wrong. If you are not certain, leave your original answer. More often than not, it will be right.

ESSAY TESTS

Most essay tests include a few objective questions. Handle these first. Spend as little time as you can on them. If an answer does not come immediately to mind, skip it and move on. **Get to the essay questions as quickly as possible** since these will carry most of the weight when it comes to your grade. Typically, the question will ask you to take a position on some topic and support it. When writing your answer, keep focused on the question and keep your thinking organized. Good organization and clear writing will make your work easy to read for the one who is grading it and can increase your score by as much as 20 points. It is often best to start by putting together a brief outline for yourself. In it state your position, the supporting points, and your conclusion. If you make these clear, writing the essay will be simple.

When you are writing your essay remember to **stick to the point.** Bring in as much information as you can that is pertinent to your argument. If you feel a certain piece of information is important, connect it to your argument in some logical manner.

The above strategy will work if you really do understand the material. But what do you do if your grasp of the material is somewhat inadequate?   In this case, your best bet is "the shotgun approach"—write down everything you know about the subject in as organized a fashion as you can. There is both an upside and a downside to this approach.

On the downside, if your teacher really reads your work carefully, it will be very clear to her that you have little idea what you're talking about. There is a chance that she might even take offense at having to read so much nonsense which does not address the point of the essay, thus grading you down even further than your lack of focus would warrant.

On the upside, what have you got to lose by writing down whatever you **do** know? The fact is that even if she does read your essay critically, **the teacher may give you credit for knowing something about the subject,** even if it wasn't the information that was asked for. This is preferable to getting no credit on a question.   More important, many teachers (particularly in college) do not actually even read the essays. They scan through them looking for important points. If they see these points referred to, they give credit. Many students get decent grades by using the shotgun method. While it's no substitute for a well organized, well thought-out essay, it is certainly better than not answering a question.

PROBLEM-ORIENTED TESTS

Approach problem-oriented tests in the same manner as you do essay tests. If short answer questions are present, do as many of these as you can in as little time as possible. **Get to the problems as quickly as possible.** Unlike essay tests, problem-oriented tests rarely give you a choice of problems to solve. You will most likely be required to do all of them. When there are less than seven problems, briefly check all the problems and do those that are easiest first. When there are more than seven problems, start with the first one. If you can do it fairly easily— do it. If you can't, skip it and go on to the next problem. Remember to show all of your work. Be as mechanical and methodical as you can be. Include all the steps so that when you review your work your thinking will be clear to you and, of greater importance, it will be clear to the grader. You will almost always get partial credit for sound mechanics, even if your answer is wrong.

Rule: *Regardless of the type of test you're taking, spend the most time on the parts of the test that are worth the most points.*

Remember to **stay focused and have fun while you're taking the test.** If you're loose, upbeat, and are a good student with a good relationship with your teacher, you can have a really good time. You can write comments to the teacher about the test as you're taking it. You can compliment him on well thought-out questions and, when you have an especially good relationship with a teacher, you can playfully get on his case if you think a question was inappropriate or too obscure. Sometimes, on questions to which you do not know the answer, you can make up some obviously wrong, yet amusing answer. I certainly do not recommend this approach for everyone. It will almost never work if your teacher believes you to be an average or poor student. It will rarely work if you do it while you're stressed out. It will usually work if you're a good student, enjoying yourself. By work, I mean you will provide your professor with a chuckle and perhaps a feeling of validation while they are grading your test, neither of which they usually experience while performing such a task.

AFTER THE TEST

Party! Enjoy yourself! Especially after big tests, finals, SATs, etc. I know most of you don't need the encouragement. It's what you do anyway. Great! Good job! Keep it up! However, some of you out there don't take the time to reward yourselves. Some of you even continue to worry. That's OK. However, you'll be better off if you do something to have a good time. Once a test is over, there isn't a lot you can do about it until you get it back so . . . **Enjoy!**

GETTING YOUR TEST BACK

When you get your test back, **first accept the grade on your paper gracefully.** This may sound trite, and yet it's very important, especially if you're going to discuss your test with the teacher. Teachers do not like angry, belligerent students, and they neither like nor respect whiners and complainers. They tend to both like and respect students who accept their grades and try to improve them intelligently. After accepting the grade, check to see if your score was added up correctly. Then go over the questions you got wrong. If, upon learning the explanation of the "right" answer, you still either do not understand it, or you feel that your answer was actually right, go and discuss it with your teacher. Be prepared to defend your answer intelligently. **If you can logically present your case for your answer's integrity and thereby demonstrate your understanding of the material, you will often get at least some extra points for your answer.** What's more, your teacher will know you understand the material and this will often be reflected on your final grade.

Again, please remember to have fun while you do this. Go to your teacher with a good attitude. More often than not students take an angry posture. They cop an attitude that says to the teacher, "You're wrong." This attitude rarely has a positive effect. While you may get the points, you will not get your teacher's good will. That good will can often be the difference between a B and an A. **Approach your professor from the position of "Let's discuss this and see what there is to learn."** Be uptone. And be as ready to accept being wrong as you are ready to demonstrate that you are right.

After you understand your mistakes and get whatever points you can, do a test analysis if necessary. How do you know its necessary? **A test analysis is necessary if you got less than an A and did not expect to.** If you went into the test believing you were prepared and got a B-, guess what? You were not adequately prepared. You need to find out why. A test analysis will often provide you with the answer and point you toward steps to correct this situation for the next test.

PREPARING FOR STANDARDIZED TESTS

Standardized tests include the SAT, NMSQT, GRE, MCAT, LSAT, GMAT, among others. As the SAT and GRE (general) are the most commonly encountered tests in this group, the discussion will be pointed towards them. You will hear, "You cannot prepare for these tests, so don't try." **This is a lie! Though preparation for these tests should really start in grade** school, a few months of focused preparation can greatly improve the scores of many *STUDENTS*.

Note to parents: Make sure your children read and that they read challenging books, magazines, etc. The more the better. Developing basic math skills from an early age is equally important.

If you are a *STUDENT* and these tests are a few years away, read. When you read, have a dictionary nearby, and use it when you encounter words you do not fully understand. In addition, if you're planning on taking a test with a math component, start a collection of flashcards with all the algebraic and geometric rules, theorems, axioms, and formulas you encounter.

If you are a *STUDENT* and are close to taking a standardized test, go to a bookstore and pick up one of the many practice guides available. Take a practice test and see where you stand. **Whether your practice score is good enough depends upon your goals.** For example, if you're planning to go to do your graduate work at an Ivy League school, you'll probably want to score 650 or better on each part of an GRE exam, on the verbal, the quantitative and the analytical. If you're a high school student and planning to go to a state school, 550 or better on each part, the verbal and the math, of an SAT exam may be adequate. To find out what scores are desirable, check out the admission requirements of the individual schools you're interested in.

Remember, **the higher your score, the greater your options.** (A word about checking out schools. **Ask for the average score of students admitted.** The university will usually give you the lowest score you need to be considered for acceptance. In highly competetive programs, rarely are students actually accepted with these scores).

If your scores need moderate improving (50-100 points/part) you may simply need to take some practice tests on your own and improve your skills. If your scores need a lot of improvement (150+ points/part), you have your work cut out for you. If you are very self-disciplined, much of this work can be done on your own. If you are not very self-disciplined, you may want to take a prep course. The particular course you take will depend on the instructor, cost, time, etc. Over the years, numbers of students have reported receiving great benefits from these courses and others report they were a complete waste of time. **My suspicion is that those students that did the work necessary outside the course were the ones that benefited.** Those that expected to sit in a room a few hours a day and significantly improve their grades were the ones that received little benefit. In general what you'll probably need to do to succeed on the SAT and the general GRE is:

1. **Put together flashcards for all the geometric and algebraic rules, theorums, etc.**
2. **Put together flashcards for lists of suffixes, prefixes, and roots**
3. **Study these cards**
4. **Read challenging books and articles for comprehension (One way to do this is to visualize what you're reading as you're reading it)**
5. **Take plenty of practice tests**

If you need to gain more than 400 points (200 on each part) on one of these tests, plan on spending about 3 hours/day 4 days/week over one summer. I know of students who improved their GRE scores by more than 600 points over their first GRE practice test by putting in about 5 hours/day,   3 days/week for an entire summer. It can be done. **Your scores can be improved.** You simply need to put in the time, doing the right work.

THE IMPORTANCE OF

STANDARDIZED TESTS

The importance of these tests cannot be over emphasized! In a system that relies so heavily on numbers, these are the most emphasized numbers there are! **In some disciplines and at some schools these tests are almost all that matter! A great score on these tests can make up for years of mediocre work!**

SAT (entrance exam for college) **GRE** (ent. exam for grad school) **GMAT** (ent. exam for grad school)

Great test scores (as well as poor scores) will work on the minds of admission committee members! Let's say your GPA is 2.65 and you get a 1500 on your SAT, GRE, or GMAT. It is likely you will be viewed as an exceptionally bright student who just wasn't motivated to do school work. It is likely you will have many college options. Conversely, let's say that your GPA is 3.5 and you get a 875 on your SAT, GRE, or GMAT. You will most likely be viewed as only an average student who attended a school with low standards and inflated grades. It is likely you will have relatively few college options.

LSAT, and **MCAT,** (ent. exams for law, medical schools)

If you excel (top 5%), on this test you are in law school or medical school—almost regardless of any other factors. If you do only well, you'll have difficulty getting into many schools, regardless of any other factors. I'll give you two examples. One student I know graduated the University of California, Berkeley (one of the best schools in the country with a 3.9 GPA.

She was active in student and community affairs. She scored in the top 20% on her LSAT. She was accepted into only one law school. Another student I know graduated UCLA with a 3.0 GPA in four years while competing on the swim team. He swam well enough to earn a gold medal in the 1988 Olympics. He went on to earn his master's degree from a top flight communications program (Syracuse). While pursuing his master's he worked with minority youth as well as fulfilled his obligations to the U.S. Olympic Committee. He is one of the most honorable and capable individuals it has been my pleasure to have known. It is obvious he will succeed at anything he sets his mind on. He too scored only in the top 20% and was accepted into only one law school.

If you know you are going to have to take any of these tests, start preparing as soon as possible. Get hold of practice tests and begin to master the skills necessary to succeed. If you need help—get it! **Excelling at these tests will open up many doors.**

RELIEVING TEST ANXIETY

Test anxiety is nothing more than your body and your mind freaking out a bit on you. It is their **response** to being in a testing situation. It is initially brought on when you pay attention to images of failure, death, destruction or other such frightening images which run through your mind before or during a test. Your body then behaves as if these images are real and starts responding as if danger is actually present. If you allow this to happen (sometimes once is enough), it becomes a habit and you find yourself experiencing an anxiety response whenever you take a test.

For the most part, changing your response to tests is a fairly straightforward procedure if you truly want to make the change. Basically it involves getting competent at controlling your mind (i.e., focusing on what you want), and getting competent at controlling your body. There are many ways to learn how to do this. People have done it through yoga, meditation, biofeedback, self-hypnosis, exercise, diet, the list goes on. The only method I would not recommend is medication, as almost all medication will hinder your performance on tests to some degree.

When developing your ability to respond the way you want, I would suggest starting with the most obvious methods first. These are diet and exercise. Many people who would ordinarily experience only a mild nervousness have this nervousness amplified as a result of their diet, rest patterns, and exercise habits. If you are one of those students that pulls all-nighters studying for tests trying to stay awake by drinking lots of coffee, cola, or by popping amphetamines, who then have test anxiety attacks and wonder why—WAKE UP BOZO!!! Caffeine, sugar, speed, and lack of sleep all greatly amplify nervousness, as well as other emotions. Remember READY? (Rested, Eaten, Alcohol, Drugs?) If you're tired or hungry or if you've had alcohol or drugs recently (yes Dear, sugar and caffeine are drugs), your ability to control your mind and body will be severely debilitated. So before you go to a psychologist, doctor, or counselor, try eating right for a month, getting plenty of sleep and exercise, then see what happens to your ability to feel the way you want to feel.

If you are already eating well, getting plenty of sleep and proper exercise, yet you still experience test anxiety, you may want to try the following exercise:

Exercise 6.2   Relaxation

1. Focus on your breathing. Begin breathing slowly and deeply (from your diaphragm, i.e., your midsection). Breath under 12 breaths per minute. To slow your breathing down, exhale by pursing your lips and slowly blowing out each breath. (If you're in the midst of an anxiety attack, doing this will often help immediately).

2. Center yourself. Bring all your attention to the here and now. Focus on your breathing. Only on your breathing. Then, focus on the form your body is in. Feel your feet on the floor, your buttocks in the chair, your hair on your head, your head on your neck, your neck on your shoulders. Do this for as long as it takes for your body to calm down.

3. Concentrate on the test material you do know.

Before trying the above relaxation exercise right before a test, practice it in a safe environment until you know you can slow your breathing down and begin to concentrate quickly (within about a minute). Then try it just before a test. This will usually be all most people need to calm themselves down so that they can perform at their best. If you still feel you need or want professional assistance, by all means go and get it. There are also plenty of books about relaxation and stress management in libraries and book stores, and I highly recommend checking some of them out. Many contain very useful tools for gaining increased self-control. Try them and see what they have to offer.

CHAPTER 7

WRITING FOR
HIGH GRADES

SOME THOUGHTS ON WRITING

Throughout your education, your performance in two activities will determine approximately 90% of your grades: 1) your performance on tests, and 2) your performance on papers. In the previous three chapters, our discussion focused on tests and test preparation. This chapter will address writing in general and the writing of academic papers in particular. Since exams often include essay questions, becoming a better writer will not only improve your performance on papers, it will benefit your performance on tests as well.

TESTS AND PAPERS

In high school you usually have little choice as to how your performance is evaluated. In college, however, you will often have the choice of taking a class in which your grade will be predominantly based on tests or a class in which your grade will depend much more upon how well you write papers. **It is very important that you are aware of this choice when it presents itself.** For instance, if you need to take a history course and two professors teach it, find what work each one requires in the course. If one assigns a paper in addition to a mid-term and final, and one requires only a mid-term and a final, you have some important information which may help your performance in the course. You can choose the professor whose requirements suit your tastes. Are you better at writing on your own chosen topic with lots of time? Take the course with the paper. Do you thrive in testing environments? Take the course with only the tests.

In order to choose effectively and wisely, you have to be competent at both. It's one thing to choose to take a test-based class rather than a writing-based class simply because you do better taking tests. It's an entirely different thing to make that choice because you know you are incompetent at writing. In fact, in the latter case you do not really have much of a choice at all. You are compelled, rather than free, to take the test-based class as a result your of writing incompetence. Although choices may be plentiful in some areas, you will have your share of required classes in which you do not have a choice of sections or professors. If these classes demand papers—you will need to be able to write good papers in order to get good grades.

When you have a choice, choosing tests or papers is mostly a matter of preference. Tests and papers are quite different. **Tests most often require a little knowledge about a lot of information. Papers require a lot of knowledge about a little information.** You will tend to retain more knowledge, for a longer period of time, when you write a paper. Why? Remember the chapter on memory? Papers require much more encoding activity. You often drastically alter the form of the information as you write. Writing is quite a step beyond outlining.

THE VALUE OF WRITING WELL

To write a good paper or essay you have to write clearly, concisely, and in an organized manner. If you write well you will clarify your thinking and increase your understanding of your subject. If you write well you have an advantage when it comes to being graded on essay tests as well as papers. **A paper that is well written, even if it is off the mark, will often get a higher grade than one that is poorly written, yet makes a good point.** The same goes for many essay tests. In college I took a literature class with one of my friends. We had to write a single paper, about 20 pages long, for our grade. She did not write her paper on the assigned subject or in the assigned style—she wasn't even close. She told me she simply did not want to write about the subject the way the professor wanted. When we got our papers back she had received an A with a note from the professor saying, "This was not the assignment! However, it was so well written that I just had to give you an A." A well written paper or essay will often get a good grade, regardless of the content!

IMPROVING YOUR WRITING

There are a number of ways to improve your writing. Most colleges and universities have writing classes and/or laboratories for just this purpose. They can be of great benefit to those students who lack the writing skills necessary to succeed at the college level. They can also benefit those who have the skills and don't know that they do. Having your writing validated may be all that you need to become confident in your abilities. In these writing classes and labs you do what you need to do most in order to improve your writing skill— you write. You write about many subjects, in many styles. For those who need to improve their writing, these classes and labs provide a great opportunity .

Another way to improve your writing is to read academic papers written by other students. These can serve as models for your own work. Ask your professor for these models or check the library to see if they are available. When you get them pay attention to their form and structure. Use them as skeleton formats for your own papers. Keep using them until you have developed your own, successful, style.

ASSIGNMENTS AREN'T ALWAYS WHAT THEY SEEM

What happens if you want to write a paper which meets your needs, yet your interests do not seem to meet the requirements of the assignment? Assignments aren't always what they seem! **You can write about almost anything as long as you can demonstrate the relevance of your idea to your teacher** (this means that you discuss your ideas with your teacher <u>before</u> you begin to write your paper). For example, imagine that you're a philosophy major taking a class in twentieth-century literature to fulfill an area requirement. Your assignment is to write a criticism of Hemingway's novel, <u>A Farewell to Arms</u>. The novel itself doesn't really interest you. However, you are interested in how Hemingway's writing is consistent with the philosophy of Existentialism— Existentialism happens to be the focus of your work in philosophy. (Existentialism is a philosophy emphasizing that humans are responsible for their own actions and free to choose their development and destiny.) You could write a paper discussing how in this one work Hemingway appears to be an existentialist. The work you do for such a paper might be applicable to your future work in philosophy. You may even be able to use the paper, or some of the points you make in it, in another class. If you show real interest in a particular project, teachers will almost always let you pursue your interest. Remember, **it's your education. Tailor assignments to meet your needs.**

TYPES OF WRITING ASSIGNMENTS

During the course of your studies you will likely encounter three types of writing assignments:

1. **creative writing assignments**
2. **scientific research papers**
3. **liberal arts research papers**

Regardless of which type of writing assignment you have, it often will pay to meet with your professor and talk over the assignment. Such a meeting may give you a better sense for what she expects. Also, if you're having some difficulty deciding what to write about , she can help you.

WRITING CREATIVE WRITING ASSIGNMENTS

Creative assignments include writing short stories, plays, poetry, etc. These require little or no formal research. **In these assignments you will most often find your writing style and your command of the language to be the key factors in your grade, followed by creativity and demonstrated personal growth.** If you simply like writing, these assignments can be a whole lot of fun. They really allow you to play with the language and express yourself.

The single most efficient way to develop your creative writing ability is to read a variety of literature and consciously imitate the styles of writers that you admire. As you develop your style develop your descriptive vocabulary, active verbs, adverbs, and adjectives that appeals to the senses. A good creative writer doesn't tell her reader what is happening, **she shows her reader what is happening.**

There is always a subjective component involved in the grading of any writing assignment. This component is often the dominant one in creative writing assignments. Therefore, the single most efficient way to get good grades in many creative writing classes is to discover the writers your instructor most admires and to imitate them. Even better, do your best to determine the writing of your style of your instructor and imitate that. (Many creative writing instructors are insecure and give the best grades to STUDENTS who seem to idolize them.)

WRITING SCIENTIFIC RESEARCH PAPERS

Scientific research papers report the results of new experiments—most often experiments you have performed yourself. If you are majoring in a science or a social science you most likely will have to write at least one scientific paper. The particular form your paper will take will vary according to your particular field. While each discipline has its own conventions, almost all scientific research papers follow a similar general format consisting of four sections:

1. an introduction
2. a description of your method
3. an analysis of your results
4. a conclusion

The introduction generally consists of a literature review in which you discuss the past research that has led up to your present work. You need to show how your work logically follows from the work of the scientists who have come before you. At the end of your introductory section, you present your hypothesis. **Your hypothesis is simply your prediction about the outcome of your experiment.** For example, if you are conducting an experiment to determine the best kind of food to eat before a test, your hypothesis might be "Students perform best on tests when they eat junk food the night before." Often the introduction is the longest of the four sections.

In the section describing your method, you tell your reader how you will test your hypothesis. How will you select your subjects? Will they be volunteers or will you pay them? Will they all be freshman or will they be a cross section of students? To what experimental conditions will they be assigned? The night before tests, will some eat junk food, while others eat pasta, and still others eat meat? Will all your subjects eat their meals at different times? Once selected, how will they proceed through your experiment? What will they do, exactly? The answers to these and many other questions are part of the method section.

In the analysis section, you discuss the way you analyzed the data your experiment produced and state the results of that analysis. Which group actually performed the best on their tests? How do you know?

In your conclusion, you discuss your results. Did they support your hypothesis? What should students eat the night before tests in to assure their best performance? Does it matter? How do your results augment the work of other scientists? Was your research consistent with what others would have predicted, or do your results fly in the face of past findings? Your conclusion should sum up the significance of your research.

A typical scientific research paper follows the format outlined above. Again, the specifics will vary with the discipline, and the format will basically remain the same.

LIBERAL ARTS RESEARCH PAPERS

Analytical research papers are the type you will encounter the most throughout your educational experience. Typical college research papers are all analytical in nature. **They require you to state your opinion about a topic and present arguments to support that opinion—arguments based on valid evidence and logic.** They are not reports. Reports simply review what happened, when, and to whom. For instance, if the subject you're about to write on is the American revolution and you decide to write about where and when the major battles took place—this is a report. The result of such a paper would be a recap of the main battles, "so-and-so did this and such-and-such happened." This is not an analytical paper. An analytical paper would make a claim such as the results of two battles determined the outcome of the war—a matter of opinion.

WRITING A LIBERAL ARTS

RESEARCH PAPER

The point of writing a research paper is to convince a professor that you are an independent thinker capable of formulating a viewpoint on your own from existing information. In order to convince him that you excel at doing the above and that you therefore deserve a superior grade, he needs to see the workings of your thought process. When professors grade papers closely, they play Devil's Advocate— they question every one of your arguments. Therefore, make sure that you make neither "sweeping generalizations" nor assertions that you don't back up with evidence. Make sure your arguments are well supported and reasonable.

There are five steps to writing a typical liberal arts research paper:

1. Choosing your topic
2. Formulating your thesis
3. Doing your research
4. Writing your paper
5. Presenting your work

CHOOSING YOUR TOPIC: FOCUSING YOUR WORK

Choosing a topic is the first—and most critical—part of the writing process. **If you do this well you can save yourself a great deal of time and work** as well as provide yourself with a rewarding experience. The first question to ask yourself is, "Am I interested in the subject?" If you answered "yes," then ask yourself, "What about the subject would I be most interested in learning more about?" The answer will lead you to your topic. You see, interest is the most relevant criterion when choosing a paper topic. If you are really and truly interested in a subject— have at it! Your chances of writing a good paper increase when you bring genuine enthusiasm to your research. Expect to spend more time than usual doing your work though, as interest often demands it. However, you can also expect to enjoy your research!

If you answered the first question, "No, I am not interested in the subject," let the games begin! This is where taking the right attitude can really make a difference. **The goal now becomes to do the best possible paper in the least amount of time.**

A number of questions may help lead you to your paper topic if you're not interested in the overall subject. First ask yourself, "What do I already know about?" If there is an area in which you have already accumulated a fair amount of knowledge, consider tying your area of expertise into the subject matter at hand in some fashion. Even better: "**Do I have any papers I could modify and use for this assignment?**" If you've already written something related to the subject, you may be able to reuse that paper as is or modify it to fit the assignment. Please beware! Sometimes modifying an old paper can take longer than writing a new one. Use your best judgment. I know of one *STUDENT* who successfully used the same paper for three different classes. One of my best friends actually used a paper he wrote in seventh grade for a college history course (he only had to upgrade some of the vocabulary). He received an A both times.

The most skilled *STUDENTS* always ask themselves, "**How can this assignment benefit me in the future?**" This is an excellent question. They are not only looking down the road for opportunities to use their work again, they are looking toward larger projects. Some of you that are in college may be aiming to do a senior thesis as a final project. This is usually a major work. Often, much of the work that you do throughout your schooling can be applied to this project. Take every opportunity to make your work count for as much as possible. For example, if you're planning to do a thesis on Russian literature, your history papers could explore facets of Russian history or the history of Russian literature. Your psychology papers could deal with famous Russian psychologists or with the psychological profile of a significant Russian novelist. Science papers could criticize the work of Russian scientists. Get the picture? After two or three years of focusing your work in this manner, much of your senior project would be done before you would even need to start work on it. **The** farther into the future you can see, the more focused—and therefor useful—your work will be.

CHOOSING YOUR TOPIC:

QUESTIONS AND RELATIONSHIPS

A topic is a relevant idea expressed in terms of an open-ended question. For a question to be open-ended, its answer needs to be expressed as an arguable opinion—an opinion with no definitive answer. "How much foreign aid did the colonists receive, and from whom did they receive it?" is an example of a close-ended question—one that would not be a suitable paper topic. There is a definitive answer to it. You cannot argue it. The colonists received X amount of aid from Y countries. End of story. "What was the value of foreign aid to the colonists war effort?" is an example of an open-ended question. There is no simple yes/no, right/wrong answer to it. Given the proper research, you could make a case for a number of answers.

For a topic to be a good one, it has to be relevant—it has to relate, in some way, to the subject you're studying. While a relationship may be somewhat tenuous or far-flung, if you can see the relationship, you can generate a topic. Your papers are only as good as the topics you choose to write about. The sooner you become proficient at generating interesting, relevant topics, the sooner your paper writing will improve.

Generating a topic is a matter of observing relationships or connections. In one sense everything can be seen as being interrelated. Chairs are related to table and desks. This is easy to see. Chairs are also related to windows and walls. Can you see these connections? Chairs can also be related to aardvarks, yodeling, and sleeping bags. Can you make these connections? Use your imagination. Granted some of these connections may seem more tenuous than others, but you can still make them. The following exercise is designed to help you increase your ability to see relationships and create connections.

Exercise 7.1 Creating relationships

1. *Pick two items and write down how they are related.*
2. *Start with closely related pairs (e.g., an oven and food, books and pens). When you can do this easily, go on to working with more distantly related pairs.*
3. *Keep practicing until you can create five ways any item is related to any other item. (Have fun with this exercise. You will know you are doing it right if you are amusing yourself while you're doing it.)*

Some examples: The space program and apple sauce. Shakespeare and Grizzly bears. Feel free to get as wild as you like. Relate three items instead of two. **Enjoy!** You may be asking yourself, "What is the practical application of this exercise?" Simply doing this exercise will allow you to see connections you've never seen before. With practice, you will gain the ability to look at the world in a different and more creative way, and it is **from unusual perspectives that interesting topics are generated.**

In 1988 I first introduced this exercise to my students. At the time one of my students was having trouble in her economics class. Her teacher said her papers were unimaginative and did not really say much, and she had been earning C's. She worked for about 15 minutes on this exercise until she became consciously competent at creating connections. The next economics paper she wrote was on the similarities between market-based economics and the mating habits of the praying mantis. She got a B on that paper. This exercise helped her, as it can help you, see interesting parallels and expand your horizons.

FORMULATING YOUR THESIS

Your thesis is simply your opinion boiled down to one arguable statement. If your topic question is "What was the value of foreign aid to the American colonists' war effort?," your thesis would be your answer—phrased in a single arguable statement. One possible thesis statement: "The colonists' war effort would still have succeeded without foreign aid from sympathetic nations. Or: "The value of foreign aid to the American colonists' war effort was largely psychological." Or: "America would still be a British colony without the aid the colonists received from other nations." All these statements are arguable. They are all valid theses.

Theses are typically generated **from your research, from your own beliefs, or from some combination of the two.** Often, you formulate your thesis while you're researching your topic: you will probably observe a common thread woven through your readings; you may notice there is weak evidence for a commonly held belief, you may find gaps in a certain author's arguments, you may find evidence again and again supporting a particular viewpoint. Sometimes you first formulate your thesis based upon your own beliefs. If you have a strongly held opinion about a particular issue, you can decide to use that as your thesis. If you're writing a paper in economics and you believe legalizing drugs will have a positive effect on the health of the United States' economy, you have a thesis.

Regardless of how you arrive at your thesis, your next job is to find the evidence to prove your point.

DOING YOUR RESEARCH

As the Age of Information progresses, some aspects of doing research are getting very easy while at least one aspect is getting more difficult. Research involves gathering information from a number of sources and extracting what you need in order to develop a thesis about your topic and defend it.

Gathering information is amazingly simple and will continue to get simpler. Only ten years ago students had to go to the <u>Readers Guide to Periodical Literature</u> or to abstracts and manually sift through them, a year at a time, to pull out articles relevant to their topics. Now almost all recent writings (usually for about the last 8-15 years) can be obtained by subject through computer database systems in university libraries. Information that used to take days to accumulate now can take as little as an hour to find. To gain access to these systems, **GET TO KNOW YOUR LIBRARY!** Learn what it has to offer. Taking the time to learn how easy it is to get information that you want will save you weeks of work and provide you with tools you can use to greatly enhance the quality of your work. Simply go to any librarian and ask for help. **Most librarians are godsends.** Treat them accordingly. They can make your work much, much easier and much, much better.

As gathering information gets easier, sifting through all that information to get what you want is becoming more difficult, if for no other reason than that the quantity of information available is increasing. **The way to wade through this morass of information is to know exactly what you are looking for.** This is called "goal-oriented reading." The better you can narrow down the information you need, the faster you will get it. Once you have your needs narrowed down, learn to read only for that information. **You almost never need to read whole books, chapters, or articles. You simply have to extract the information you need from them.** For example, if you're doing a report on world literacy and you're reading a book on literacy, go to the index, find the pages on "world literacy," and only read the parts that are applicable.

If you've already decided on a thesis and you're searching for ammunition in support of it, just skim the pages for that information. This can save you a lot time. You will learn very quickly if your thesis is supportable or not. If ammunition in support of your thesis is hard to come by, yet lots is available against it, you may be wise to change your thesis to one that is easier to support. If you haven't decided on a thesis, you can skim through your sources to find one that will be easy to defend.

Whether you begin with your thesis formulated or not, make note of all the information you find on both sides of the issue you working with. You will need to include all sides of the argument in your paper. If you only present arguments in favor of your position, your professor may very well crucify you. In the body of your paper you will need to present the best arguments the other side has to offer and refute them as well as presenting the best arguments your side has to offer.

Two specific short cuts:

1. **If you have an assignment that requires that you read three articles, chose short articles.**
2. **If you are using abstracts to locate possible sources of information and the information you need is in the abstract, just use the abstract.**

These are just two shortcuts. There are others. As you progress through your education, do so with an eye to developing your own.

Once you have found the information you are after, write it down. Many students prefer using cards to record this information; others prefer standard paper. I recommend index cards as they make it easier to organize and reorganize your work later on. If you use index cards, keep it simple—one point to a card. If you use paper, make sure you only write on one side. (You may need to see all your notes at once at some point.) Whichever method you choose, make sure you take down the necessary bibliographic information: title of book or article, journal (if applicable), author, publication date, and page number. Also, make sure you quote accurately.

Your research is complete when you have your thesis and list of arguments both attacking and defending it. If you've done your research well, writing your paper will be relatively simple.

WRITING YOUR PAPER: ORGANIZATION

After you've done your research, the next step is to organize and outline your paper. All liberal arts research papers are organized into three parts:

1. A beginning
2. A middle
3. An end

It is your job to make sure the reader knows which part he is reading.

THE BEGINNING: THE INTRODUCTION AND THESIS

The purpose of the introduction is three-fold: 1) to give the readers the necessary background for them to understand the issue you're about to present, 2) to grab the readers' interest, and 3) to state your thesis. Your introduction should be very brief in comparison with the rest of your paper. For instance, if your paper will be about 3 pages long, your introduction should be one short paragraph. If you're writing a 30-page paper, your introduction should not be more than 3 pages. In a small amount of space you have to tell the readers what they're about to read, motivate them to read it, and let them know your opinion. The readers you most care about, of course, are your professors, and they want to know "What's your point?" and "Why?" You need to tell them right at the beginning.

THE MIDDLE: THE BODY

The body should make up the largest portion of your paper. **In it you present your arguments to prove your point. To do** this job well, you must not only present your side, you must present the other side and refute it. To write a strong body of a paper, first present two or three arguments against your position, arguing each one down as you present it. After you have presented and dealt with the opposition, continue presenting evidence in support of your thesis. When presenting the rest of your arguments it is crucial that you present your second strongest point first and your strongest point last. We humans remember most what we last perceive and what we first perceive; we remember the middle the least. So start and finish the defense of your position playing to your strengths.

THE END: THE CONCLUSION

At the conclusion of your paper you sum up your arguments, bring those arguments to their logical conclusion by restating your thesis, and then exit gracefully, and—if possible—eloquently. This section too, is brief in comparison with the rest of the paper. Typically it is about the same length and often briefer than the introduction.

WRITING YOUR PAPER: ACTUALLY WRITING

You will do well to have an outline for each of these three sections. Outlines can range from being brief to in-depth. The amount of outlining you need to do is the amount it will take you to get a clear idea of how you're going to write your paper. This varies greatly among students. Some need only the briefest of sketches in order to organize their thoughts, others need outlines that resemble full-blown papers without the punctuation. You need an outline detailed enough for you to begin to write easily.

Once your outlining is complete and you know what you want to say in the order you want to say it, you're ready to write your paper. From this point on, writing should be fairly easy. **Begin by simply following your outline and continue until you have your first draft.** If you like what you've written, proofread it for grammar and spelling, make the necessary corrections and you're done writing. If you're not quite satisfied, edit your paper. (This might include adding and subtracting material, changing the wording of a particular sentence or the organization of a particular section.) **Only make those changes that you believe will substantially improve your paper.** Finish off by proofreading your work. To proofread for grammar, read your paper out loud. To proofread for spelling, go through your paper backward.

PRESENTING YOUR WORK: NEATNESS COUNTS!

I will conclude this discussion on writing with a few words about presentation. **Presentation is important. The larger the class you're in, the more important it becomes.** Teachers will usually not grade forty papers as carefully as they will grade ten. In major universities where class sizes can number in the hundreds, those who grade papers do not do so very thoroughly. Under these circumstances, papers that look good almost invariably get better grades. And even though teachers pay closer attention to the content of papers in classes that are smaller and for assignments that represent a major portion of your grade, presentation still communicates to them your intelligence (inferred from your attention to correct form, spelling, and grammar), and how much you care about your work (always an important factor to teachers in evaluating their students' work).

As a college instructor I have seen my share of papers in which it was obvious the students spent more time on their presentation than on their thinking. I, as do many other instructors, take offense at this approach; just as we take offense at carelessly presented papers, even if they do have some good ideas. **The strongest approach you can take is to present the best work you possibly can in the best manner you possibly can.**

Know and follow the standard conventions for writing papers. These include spacing (double spaced), headings (name and number on every page), correct presentation of footnotes, citations, quotations, bibliography, etc. This may sound like a lot, but once you learn the rules they will be easy to use. You can find these and the other standard conventions in <u>A Manual for Writings of Term Papers, Theses, and Dissertations</u> by Kate L. Turabian, as well as many other source books.

Here are a few tips on presentation. **Learn to type. Learn to type. Learn to type.** Even better—learn to use a word-processor, and find a way to gain easy access to one. It is much, much easier to edit and rewrite papers with a word-processor than it is with a typewriter. It is also much easier to present good-looking work. Using a word-processor will save you large amounts of time and possibly money. Many college professors will accept only typed or word-processed work. If you can buy a computer—do so. You should be able to get yourself a decent computer and printer for under $1,000.00, new; and under $600.00, used. While most colleges nowadays provide their students with access to word processing facilities, you will be better off with your own, if you can work this out. If you can't get access to a word processor, get a typewriter. If this is not possible, learn to print beautifully.

CHAPTER 8

RELATIONSHIPS:

THE POLITICS OF
EDUCATION

There are four types of relationships which significantly influence your success in school. They are your relationships with

1) **your teachers**
2) **your parents**
3) **your school**
4) **your friends**

In this chapter we will look at some of the things it takes to make these relationships work. For the purposes of this discussion **"making a relationship work" means doing what you can do to help all those involved in the relationship get what they want from it.** The more the participants get what they want, the better the relationship works. This is really a simple concept. For example, your parents want you to get good grades and you want to party. To make this relationship work, you have to set things up so you get good grades and you have time to party. Here's another: Your teacher wants you to learn about the American revolution and you're really interested in modern-day France. Study the effects France's participation in the American revolution had on modern day France. In both cases, both participants get what they want.

MAKING RELATIONSHIPS WORK

The two key factors that underlie good working relationships are responsibility and communication. The more responsible you are for your actions and the better you communicate, the more goodwill you accumulate and the better your relationships will work.

RESPONSIBILITY

Do what you do and accept the penalties and rewards for your actions. What this boils down to is **do the best work you can possibly do and accept the results.** If you did the best you can do on an assignment and got a C, accept it, then find out what it takes to improve and get to work. If you didn't do the best work you can do and got a C—tough. If you want a higher grade, do better next time. Taking responsibility is an especially important factor in developing strong relationships with teachers.

COMMUNICATION

To put it simply, **all problems, disagreements, arguments, etc. can be resolved by communicating honestly and accurately.** Almost all of the guidelines for relating well with teachers and parents involve getting into communication with them.

GOODWILL

Goodwill refers to how much support you have earned from others. **It's generally a reflection of the quality of your behavior.** Goodwill can often mean the difference between earning a B and a C. Goodwill is also often the difference between getting your financial aid application reviewed on time (after you finished it late) or not. Goodwill seems to go beyond whether a person likes you. It has to do with respect. If you earn another's respect, you often earn their goodwill. This is why responsibility and communication are so important. **We tend to respect those who take responsibility** for their actions and those who communicate truthfully. A person who admits to making a mistake is given much more respect than one who shucks and jives in an effort to cover it up.

CHEATING

Up to now I have made no mention of cheating as a way to get good grades. Cheating involves passing someone else's work off as your own. Yes, there are a myriad of ways to cheat on tests. Yes, you can go through school buying all your papers. Yes, you can go through school never doing any work. However before you decide to cheat, please understand the cost. In this universe you rarely, if ever, get something for nothing. If you get caught, the cost is not only failing an assignment or a class. That's the least of the costs you pay. The big cost is a loss of any goodwill you have accrued as well as a gain of ill-will. **You will have established a reputation that will be very difficult to overcome.** If you're a known cheater and have a borderline B, the teacher will likely give you a C. If you're a known cheater and decide to bust your tail, work hard, and so improve your grades, teachers and students will not be inclined to believe you actually did the work. In fact, they will most likely believe your good grades, no matter how honestly earned, are a result of cheating.

If, on the other hand, you do not get caught, the costs are often even higher. Sooner or later you will be asked to do your own work. When it becomes apparent that you are incompetent, you will be damaged professionally—and now we're talking money. Perhaps the biggest cost of all is your happiness and peace of mind. We live in a society where cheating, in all of its many forms, is viewed as an acceptable way to obtain material wealth. We also live in a society in which the great majority of its members are unhappy, neurotic, depressed, and stressed-out. **It is almost impossible to gain health, happiness, and peace of mind by ripping others off.** Before you decide to cheat—ask yourself, "Is it really worth it?"

THE *STUDENT* / TEACHER RELATIONSHIP

TAKING RESPONSIBILITY

As a *STUDENT* your prime responsibility is to learn. **If you do not learn it is no one's fault but your own.** If you accept this viewpoint, your chances for success are much better. Think of schooling like athletics. Coaches can show athletes how to run faster, jump higher, and get stronger. However, if you are in fact, going to run faster, jump higher, and get stronger, you are the one that needs to put time in on the track and in the weight room. The classroom is no different. If you are going to do well in class, it is you who has to do the work. If you need help, ask for it. There are usually plenty of people (parents, teachers, students) around that will help you. **Most teachers will bend over backwards to help you if you show them you are willing to take responsibility and do the work.**

DEALING WITH INSTRUCTIONS

Every time a teacher gives you an assignment, you have a choice. "Am I going to do it, or not?" It is usually in your best interest to choose to "do it." If the assignment seems out-of-line, get into communication with the teacher and find out his reasoning. If the assignment conflicts with your moral values, discuss this with your parents and friends, as well as the teacher, and work out some resolution that will satisfy the needs of all concerned. If you know of a better way to achieve the result the teacher is after, talk to her. Also, see the previous chapter on changing assignments.

TIMING

Good timing will earn you goodwill points. Teachers usually hate late work. (Why they even accept it is a mystery to me.) If you must turn in a late assignment, however, you can still make it work for you. **You can do this by taking responsibility for your lateness.** Offer no excuses. Accept whatever penalties there are graciously. Look for no special considerations. Simply apologize for being late and say it was your mistake. Do not blame it on the dog, a death in the family, or a strange illness. **Take the attitude "there are no excuses."** This will earn you your teacher's respect and goodwill. Oh, and next time, get your assignment in on time!

IMPROVING YOUR GRADES: WORKING

Before you go and ask your teacher what you can do to improve your grade, check your responsibility factor and your goodwill factor. **If you have done the best work you can do,** handed in your assignments on time, and sincerely wish to do extra work to improve your grade, go see if there's anything you can do. The earlier in the semester you do this the more amenable your teacher will be to giving you extra-credit work. Once you get the opportunity, decide whether or not it is worth it before you agree to do the work.

HAVING TROUBLE?

Along with the above guidelines, if you are having trouble in class and are going to talk to your teacher—**focus on what you can do to improve.** Many students use this time to whine or complain. This approach will yield ill-will points. If you make no excuses other than you're "having trouble" or you "don't understand" and you focus on improving, you will earn goodwill credit.

If you are having trouble understanding the material, one of the best questions you can ask your instructor is, "What about this subject is so simple and obvious that you might have overlooked mentioning it?" Often instructors have been working with their material for so long that they lose touch with what it's like to be a new student. This question may help them get back in touch with that viewpoint.

IMPROVING? YOUR GRADES: BEGGING

There is nothing so utterly revolting and obnoxious as a student begging for grades. This involves any activity to get the teacher to give you a good grade other than honest work and demonstration of ability. Begging usually is delivered as a whining, sniveling plea for mercy. "If I don't get a B in the course, I can't be a psychology major" or "If I don't pass this class, my parents will kill me." As a teacher the only thing that keeps me from actually killing a student who pulls this is the inconvenience such an action would cost me. Most teachers feel similarly, though many do not express these feelings overtly. My usual response to such an approach: "If you do B work, I'll give you a B." **Understand, that in my book there is nothing, absolutely nothing, you could do to earn more ill-will than begging.**

IMPROVING YOUR GRADES: ARGUING

Arguing is great—done in the right spirit. **If you can demonstrate you know the material—go for it.** Usually this happens after tests (see the section on what to do after a test). Most teachers love a well thought-out academic argument. By the way, an argument in this context does not mean a "fight." It means a clarification. These arguments can be calm, heated, and/or anywhere in between. The key is that you are demonstrating your understanding. If your understanding is adequate, you will get the test points and goodwill. If your argument is weak and you accept your defeat with style and grace, you will at least earn goodwill credit.

TALKING

Talk with your professors outside of class. Discuss your ideas with them and ask them about their ideas, their interests, and their work. **Take a genuine interest in them.** Teachers are humans too. Like most of us they love talking about themselves and their interests. Establishing a personal rapport with your teachers and caring about them will earn you much goodwill—if its done genuinely. It will also give you insights into their priorities which may prove very useful.

THE TEACHER / *STUDENT* RELATIONSHIP

If there are any teachers or teachers to be reading this book, here are a few guidelines that may help you make your work more fulfilling.

RESPONSIBILITY

Know what you are responsible for. **You are responsible for providing the best opportunity you can for your students to learn.** You are not responsible for their learning; you are responsible for the quality of opportunity you provide. Whether or not a particular student takes advantage of that opportunity is his business. However, if most of your students aren't learning—it most likely is your business. Do everything you can to discover the reasons and make the necessary corrections.

CLASS RULES

Set down your rules, make sure they're understood, get your students' agreement to them, and stick to them. If you really want to help your students grow up, this is critical.

Regarding assignments, papers, tests, etc., I have found the "no excuses" approach to work best. Its clean, clear, and easily understood.   It relieves you of the task of deciding which excuses are valid and which are not.   Once students actually believe you're serious, they begin to enjoy the discipline of it.

CRITICISM/FEEDBACK

Critique your students' work properly. First, tell them what they did right and validate them.   Second, point out their mistakes and problem areas.   Finally, show them how they can improve their work.

THE *STUDENT* / PARENT

RELATIONSHIP

To make these relationships work it's the *STUDENT*'s responsibility to keep in touch. **Let your parents know what is going on. Be as honest and as accurate as you can.** Talk to them about your goals and plans. Let them know how you are doing in your classes. Discuss what you are learning with them. (Remember—teaching is a form of active encoding; use your parents as students.) Let them know what you need.

THE PARENT / *STUDENT* RELATIONSHIP

SUPPORT

As a parent, your primary role is a supportive one. **You are responsible for providing the best environment you can in which your children can learn.** Within this environment, school has to be the number one priority. You have to demonstrate this through your deeds as well as your words. Homework comes first, family chores second. Make sure your children have adequate time and space to study. When they are working, handle all their phone calls for them—take messages. Do not under any circumstance disturb them while they are working. This will help them concentrate on the tasks at hand. Also, make sure brothers and sisters know the importance of supporting each other when they are working. Lead by example.

THROW OUT THE T.V.

One of the best actions you can take in support of your children's education is to throw out (or at least lock up) the television(s) in your home. **There is no other object in the average person's environment that is more harmful to their growth.** Television is debilitating in a number of ways. Most obvious: time spent watching T.V. is time not spent doing other—constructive—things. Not as obvious, though every bit as real: television destroys creativity and inquisitiveness by demanding nothing from the viewer. Even less obvious, though more insidious: television allows the bean counters to push their values onto your children. More and more the bean counters, through television, are determining the ethical character of our society. If you are not aware of this, **the ethic that they preach with greatest vigor is "Your worth is determined by what you have—not by what you do or what you are. So, BUY, BUY, BUY!** This usurped ethic is ravaging our country!

Although television can be a wonderful educational tool (witness Sesame Street), it rarely reaches for lofty heights. The bulk of its programming is simply garbage. As awful as most of television's offerings are, it is not in these offerings that the real danger lies. **Television's real danger lies in its addictiveness. We are addicted to it.** The average American household has its television on 6-to-8 hours a day! Think about it. If you work 8 hours a day and sleep 8 hours a day, then most of your free time is spent in front of the tube. **If you think you and you family aren't hooked, try to go a week without television, and see what happens.**

Because of these damaging qualities of the medium (and we haven't even begun to discuss television's effects on familial relationships), **it is critical that you take control of the viewing habits of your household.** Some suggestions include: limiting the amount of time your children can watch T.V. recreationally to 1 hr/day, 2hrs/day on weekends and holidays; watching quality educational shows as a family; and controling all access to the T.V.—there should almost never be a television kept in your childrens' rooms. **Taking measures such as these can greatly improve the quality of your family's life!**

BE INTERESTED

Be interested in what your children are doing in school. **Provide them with opportunities to teach you what they have** learned. Know your children's goals and plans and focus on them. If a problem arises, handle it and refocus on the goal. Know what assignments they have and when they are due. Talk with your children every day to find out how they are doing and show them you care. In some families, dinner time functions as meeting time. It is then that family members catch up on the day's events and check in with each other. Whatever time you pick, keep it consistent.

VALIDATE YOUR CHILDREN'S WORK

When your children do something well, let them know you have noticed and that you care—reward them. The bigger the win, the bigger the reward. Before you reward them find out what rewards they in fact need and want. Often a big smile and hug is much more rewarding than an expensive gift. Know what is important to your children.

CRITICISM/FEEDBACK

Critique your child's work properly. First, tell them what they did right and validate them. Then point out their mistakes. Finally show them how they can correct those mistakes.

PENALTIES AND REWARDS

Accept the penalties and rewards your child accrues at school, as long as they are fair. Too often, parents interfere with their children's growth by stepping in for them and trying to mitigate the poor grades their children have earned. While it may seem as if you are helping them, you are in fact, usually stunting their growth. Children must learn that their actions have consequences. Know their teachers' rules and help your child follow them. If you have some difficulty understanding a situation, talk with the teacher.

CARE

Mostly—just **care**.

THE *STUDENT* / SCHOOL RELATIONSHIP

School relationships include those with all the people in addition to teachers that you come in contact with while doing school business: secretaries, deans, maintenance workers, principals, counselors, office staff, nurses, etc. **Respect them and show your appreciation for the work they do.**   Treat them like the valuable human beings they are. When you need their assistance, ask for it politely. After they've helped you, thank them. Know their names. Smile at them when you pass. Afford them the same courtesies you want others to afford you. I know this may all sound trite, but you might be surprised at how many students, particularly graduate students, treat the school staff as their personal servants. Respecting all people who help make your education possible, and taking a genuine interest in them as people, will reward you many times over. Talk about goodwill—these people have the power to make your educational experience hellish or heavenly.   I can't recall all the times during graduate school some staff person cut through the normal red tape to get me a piece of equipment quickly, or to push a petition through committees to help me meet some deadline (Dena, if you read this—thanks again!) All these people can make a big difference. **Treat them well and they will take care of you.**

THE PARENT / SCHOOL RELATIONSHIP

ESTABLISHING GOOD RELATIONSHIPS
WITH TEACHERS AND COUNSELORS

Your children can only benefit if you have strong working relationships with those responsible for educating them. **Quality communication is the tool that will most help you establish such relationships.** Most parents only talk to teachers and counselors when something is amiss. This is a grave mistake. It is very difficult to establish good relationships under stress. **It is much, much easier to establish good relationships when every thing is fine.** Talking with them when all is well will make talking with them when there is trouble more fruitful.

When things are going well, what do you talk about? **First and foremost, you validate the teacher's and counselor's work.** If your child is excited about a particular subject—**thank the teacher for her contribution!** If your child is improving her performance—**thank the teacher for his contribution!** If your child has been helped by his counselors—**thank them!** Thank them all and ask what you can do to help your child to further improve. These thanks can be given in the form of a phone call, a card, a short letter, anything that will express your sentiment.   Thanking these professionals, validating their work, and asking for their input will make a world of difference.   **Not only will you be helping to create a healthier learning environment for your children, you will be establishing valuable friendships that may last for a long, long time.**

KNOW THE REAL RULES OF THE SCHOOL
YOUR CHILDREN ARE ATTENDING

As in any organization there are rules and there are "rules." **As a parent it is your job to know unspoken rules of the school as well as the ones for public consumption.** Make certain you know the ins and outs of the school your children attend.   If your sons or daughters are in high school, know which classes are for college-bound students and which are not.   Learn what they can do to best prepare.   If they are in middle or elementary school, know what special classes and programs are available to them.   Your job will be easier if you have good working relationships with the staff at the school (see above).   **It is most important that you establish such a relationship with the principal and an assistant principal,** as they usually carry the most weight. In addition, talk with other parents. They can be a valuable source of inside information.

In your dealings with the school you need never feel intimidated. **The school is there to serve you and yours.** If there are ever any decisions to be made regarding your children—always, please always—get a second and third opinion. **Find out all your options.** If your child needed surgery you would seek other opinions, wouldn't you? Your child's education is no different. Your child's future is important, and decisions made while s/he is in school can affect that future.

THE SCHOOL'S RESPONSIBILITY

The responsibility of the school's administration and staff is to provide students with a place to learn and teachers with a place to teach. They are not there to make it easy or hard on students, although, as I just pointed out, they can, and often do, do both. If the doors are open, the environment clean, and the teachers supplied, the staff has done its job. Anything above that is gravy.

THE *STUDENT* / FRIEND RELATIONSHIP

Friends are people you know, like, and trust. Choose them wisely. In general, if your friends are successful, you will be also. If they get good grades, you probably will too. It is to your great advantage to hang out with people that will support your goals and make room for you to support theirs. **By the time you reach high school, your friends usually exert more influence over you than any other individual or group. Make sure that influence is in your best interest.**

CHAPTER 9

COLLEGE:

GETTING IN AND OUT WITH STYLE

I assume most of the students reading this book are either in college or planning to go to college. If you're a student and not planning to get a college degree, you probably should be. If you're a parent and aren't sure what your children are planning, make sure they are going to college. You should make it clear that as far as you're concerned they don't have a choice—they are going. They do have a choice as to which school they go to.

Why is it so important to get your college degree? Learn these numbers: 640,000; 1,300,000; and 2,000,000. **If you have a high school diploma you can expect to earn $640,000.00 during your working life. If you have a college degree you can expect to earn about $1,300,000.00 during your working life. If you have a graduate degree (e.g., Ph.D., M.D., J.D., etc.) you can expect to earn about $2,000,000 during your working life.** A college degree is worth about $650,000, a graduate degree is worth another $700,000. Also, the higher the degree you receive the more career choices you have. It's that simple. As we approach the 21st century, the gap between rich and poor is getting wider. More and more your position with respect to this gap is being determined by the degree of your education.

In this chapter we are going to discuss what it takes to get into college and strategies for getting out with a degree. As a college student, you have many more choices than you had as a high school student, hence the college arena is one where your skills as a *STUDENT* can be more fully expressed. It can be quite an exhilarating game!

GETTING IN

CHOOSING A COLLEGE

Which college should you attend? Obviously it depends upon what you want from a college. One of **the chief advantages that a college degree affords you is it opens doors.** The better reputation your college has, the more doors your degree will open, and the more easily they will open. Mind you, this door opening has little to do with the quality of education you actually receive. Doors open for two reasons:

1. **the mystique of the name of the university**
2. **the actual connections you make at a school**

Among the schools that will open the very best doors are Harvard, Yale, Princeton, and Stanford. These universities are responsible for educating many of the most powerful figures in the world. By attending and graduating from these schools you get the opportunity to establish ties with these people. In essence, you become one of them. Equally as important is the mystique these schools have with the general public. If you have an MBA from Harvard, and I have one from the University of Wisconsin, for example, and we are both applying for the same position, guess who is most likely to get the job, regardless of ability? Harvard MBA's often start at a salary 2 to 3 times that of many other MBA's, regardless of ability.

"It's not what you know, it's who you know." I'm sure most of you have heard this expression. For the most part it's true. **The better your connections—the more opportunities you have come your way.** As of 1991, of the one hundred United States Senators, thirty-three of them received their law degrees from either Harvard or Yale. Every discipline and profession has such a network. This is called the "Good Old Boy Network." (Recently, Good Old Girl Networks have been cropping up too.) If you want to be a successful filmmaker, you don't go to school in North Dakota. You go to the film school at UCLA or USC. You go where the contacts are. When deciding on a school, remember to consider your long-range goals. Select schools that will contribute to those goals.

Keep in mind though, there are major drawbacks to attending the best universities. One is the cost. A four-year education at these schools can cost as much as $100,000 (just tuition and books). Perhaps more significant is that these institutions foster an atmosphere of intense competition among their students. For many, this takes the fun out of the college experience that can, at some schools, be a blast. If, however, you thrive on such competition—go for it.

BIG AND SMALL

Another major issue in deciding upon a college is "big or small." Each variety has its advantages and disadvantages.

BIG

Big schools tend to be research universities. Academically, their advantages lie in the great variety of courses they can offer. Also, students have many opportunities to participate in state-of-the-art research in a number of fields. **The chief advantage of large universities, though, is that they offer a wide range of experiences to their students.** There are more students, often of wide ethnic diversity with whom you may interact. There are also more activities in which you may become involved, both as a spectator and as a participant.

Major universities have full intercollegiate and intramural athletic programs, as well as a wide range of multi-cultural activities including music, theatre, art, and dance.

These schools also have their disadvantages. It is easy to become lost in the system. They have large bureaucracies with large amounts of red tape. Students of average ability may find it more difficult to participate in some of the extracurricular activities because of the quantity of superior talent. These disadvantages aside, **the chief disadvantage of the large universities is academic. Though the quantity of available classes is great, the quality of education in those classes is often mediocre.** Many classes have hundreds of students. (e.g., enrollment in the General Psychology class at UCLA is typically 300 students, enrollment in the four required upper-division psychology classes is typically 200 students.) Student/professor contact is minimal. What contact there is is often solely based on the effort of the student. Many professors at these universities do not even like teaching. They are paid to do research, and their evaluations by their peers and superiors are based almost entirely on the quantity and quality of that research.

SMALL

These schools tend to be liberal arts colleges and are the antithesis of major research universities. **While they are not as diverse socially and culturally, they are often much stronger academically.** Classes are typically small. (e.g., enrollment in the General Psychology class at Reed College in Portland, Oregon is typically about 60 students, other psychology classes at the college typically have less than 15 students.) Professors get paid to teach first, do research second. Though class offerings are less abundant than at large universities, it is easier to independently pursue your own course of study at a small school. Professors not only are glad to help you do this, at many of these schools independent study is strongly encouraged. Extracurricular participation is also more readily available due to the smaller number of students on campus. Simply put, these schools are more intimate.

On the down side, many of these schools are not well known outside academia. Have you heard of Williams, Swarthmore, Pomona, or Reed? These are among the top schools in the world. The work at these schools is typically more difficult (whether this is an advantage or disadvantage is up to the reader). If you're not inclined to work a lot, it's harder to get lost in the system.

Which type of school you decide on is up to you. **If you look for them, excellent educational and social opportunities abound at any school.** You may simply have to work harder to root out the social opportunities at small colleges and the educational opportunities at larger universities. One option is to attend both types of schools. Spend your first two years at a large university and focus on the extracurricular benefits it offers, then, when you're ready to get back to work, transfer to a small liberal arts school for your remaining two years. Or you may want to spend a year or two at a small school to reap the benefits of a supportive environment, then transfer to a large university to take advantage of its name and research opportunities.

THE REQUIREMENTS

Rule: *There's always a way in, if you are willing to pay the price.*

This being said, typically schools evaluate their prospective students on four criteria:

1. GPA
2. SAT scores
3. Letters of Recommendation
4. "Other"

Almost all schools will tell you their minimum requirements for admission. Do not be misled. These minimum requirements often do not reflect the truth. **What you want to know are the typical scores of students who are accepted.** For example a school may set its minimum GPA standards at 3.0 and its SATs at 1000, however, the average student that is accepted might have a 3.5 GPA and an 1250 SAT score. Talk to the Dean of Admissions to get the real story. If you can't get it from the dean, talk to some of the students. You may also find these statistics in one of the College Guides—Baron's and Peterson's are two of the more popular ones. When looking through these books look for the "**Median**" scores. Regardless of how you get this information, make sure it's accurate.

THE BEST

In order to be considered for admission to the very best colleges and universities you need the following:

GPA: approximately 3.75
SAT: between 1300 and 1400
Recommendations: three prominent people in the
community who hold you in high regard

Other: 1) an extremely well written autobiography,
statement of purpose, or other sample of your
writing. (Make sure a competent writer edits your
work.)
2) significant participation in extracurricular
activities (e.g., holding an office in student
government, being the editor ofstudent
newspaper, participating in community
service,etc.)

With the above requirements met you should have a good
shot at getting into any college or university.

THE REST

GPA: 3.00
SAT: 1000
Recommendations: three respectable people who hold
you in high regard
Other: participation in extracurricular activities is an
advantage, though not required

With the above requirements you will be able to attend
many four-year colleges or universities. If you do not quite
meet them, you may still be accepted somewhere. If your GPA
is below 2.5 and your SATs are below 800, your chances of
getting accepted to a four-year university the traditional way
are slim (the traditional way being simply to mail in your
application and get accepted straight out of high school).

Wherever you decide to apply, make sure you apply to two
or more schools that are "safe" schools, schools you will
certainly get into (if you can), as well as schools that you
consider to be a stretch. If at all possible, visit the schools to

which you are considering applying and talk to students as well as professors. Find out if you'll like a school before you commit to it. **Gather as much information as you can before you make your decision.**

WHAT TO DO IF YOUR GRADES
ARE JUST NOT GOOD ENOUGH

If your grades are not good enough, **there are a number of avenues still open to you if you want to attend college.** The simplest avenue is to master the skills presented in this book, attend a two-year college, do your work, get good grades, and transfer to a four-year college. A more adventurous way is to go to the Dean of Admissions at the college of your choice and find out what it would take for him to admit you. Offer to write a substantial research paper (20 to 30 pages) on a topic of your choice to demonstrate to him/her that you are capable of doing college level work (provided that you, in fact, are capable). Sometimes they will let you in on probation (i.e., you will be required to meet certain standards (e.g., maintain a 3.0 GPA for your first year or two). If you have good reason to believe you can meet whatever standards are called for—go for it.

This also applies if you get rejected by your first choice the first time you apply, but you are accepted by another school. If you still want to graduate from your preferred school, do quality work your first year at the college that accepts you, then transfer. You can also go talk to the Dean of Admissions at your preferred school and see what you can work out.

If you really want in, you can get in!   Remember the position of the *STUDENT*—Do whatever is necessary to accomplish the goal.

FINANCING YOUR EDUCATION

A separate book is needed to adequately address this issue. Fortunately there are a number of good ones on the market. One of the best is <u>Bear's Guide To Finding Money For College,</u> by John Bear, Ph.D. published by Ten Speed Press in Berkeley, California (1984).   While money for undergraduate and graduate education gets increasingly difficult for the average student to get hold of, **billions of dollars in student grants and loans still go unclaimed each year.** Bear's Guide is an excellent place to start your search for these funds.

As with the requirements for getting into college, **the better your academic standing—the more money there will be available to you.** If your GPA is high, your SAT scores strong, your letters of recommendation superior, and your extracurricular work exemplary, you will have access to large amounts of money for your schooling. **In 1991, one young woman from Atlanta received $650,000 worth of scholarship and grant offers!** No, that's not a misprint. There is money out there!

GETTING OUT

Rule: *Rules are negotiable*.

There are rules and there are rules. There are the rules the school will tell you about and then there are the actual rules.

Your job is to understand the actual rules, to find out the truth about the system you are in. Once you understand the real rules look for opportunities to use the system to your advantage. Here are some examples from the school I attended:

ON PREREQUISITES

WHAT THEY SAID:

Prerequisites are courses the university says you need to take before you take some other courses. Usually they are lower level courses that you are required to take prior to upper level courses. For example at my school General Psychology was required before you took any other psychology course.

WHAT WAS TRUE:

Prerequisite requirements were never enforced. General Psych was in fact the last psychology course I took. Where they are enforced, professors can override them. Prerequisites are best used as guidelines. If you can handle a course without the prerequisite—have at it.

ON DECLARING A MAJOR

WHAT THEY SAID:

Most students declare a major by their junior year. You should declare a major as soon as you decide what that will be.

WHAT WAS TRUE:

At my school you did not actually have to declare your major until you were ready to graduate. In fact, declaring a major worked against you. Along with their students names, professors got a listing of their students' majors. Typically professors expected more from the students who were majoring in their area (Psych profs expected more from Psych majors) and at times graded accordingly. In my case, it was to my advantage not to declare my major until I was through with my coursework.

ON SELECTING A MAJOR

WHAT THEY SAID:

In your school catalogue there is a list of majors and the requirements to complete them. These are the options available.

WHAT WAS TRUE:

In many, if not all, schools a student can design his/her own major. If you are interested in a particular cross-disciplinary course of study, the likelihood is that you can tailor a major to your interests. This can truly be one of the most rewarding educational experiences. It allows you to focus your attention on subjects that you are actually interested in. If you structure your program right, you can apply your undergraduate work to your graduate work. You may even wind up with the introduction to your dissertation, thus saving yourself up to two years of work! To do this, find a professor who is willing to support and guide you, write up a proposal, then negotiate with the administration. (Ask your professor where to start.)

ON GENERAL COURSE REQUIREMENTS

WHAT THEY SAID:

Students are given a list of course requirements and told they have to be met.

WHAT WAS TRUE:

These requirements are often flexible. Sometimes they can be waived altogether. Often you can substitute courses or outline work in lieu of them. Write up a proposal and discuss it, in person, with whomever has the power to approve it. If your argument is strong you have a good chance to succeed.

Look into testing out of courses as another way around requirements. If you know the work and feel you can pass a test, try it. Usually there is nothing to lose. The worst that could happen is you do not pass the test and have to take the course anyway. Often all you need is the professor's approval to do this.

Rule: *Negotiate only with those who have the power to approve your plan.*

This is critical! Many people can say no, only a few (sometimes only one) can say yes. **When attempting to cut a deal, locate the person who can say yes and deal with him or her.** To find out, start by asking, "Who can approve this proposal?" and set up an appointment.

RANDOM TIPS ON PLAYING THE GAME

* Have fun and enjoy yourself—college should be a great experience!

* Start slowly. In your first quarter, take classes that you like. Don't worry about requirements or majors. Any class you take will fulfill some requirement. Use your first quarter to get settled in.

* At some time late in your first year or early in your second year take a "killer" course, whether you need it or not. Physics, chemistry, or some heavy writing course will do. This will stretch your limits and give you a different perspective on your other courses. Most of your courses will seem easy by comparison.

* If you're thinking of going to graduate school (and many of you should be), do research. It looks great on your transcript. If you work it out right you may even be able to get a publication out of it.

* Know your school's policy on failing classes. Often you can take them over again and erase an F from your transcript. If this is the case, taking an F will at times make sense. (e.g., If you're getting a C or D in a subject in your major area, take an F, take the class over and go for a higher grade.)

* Complete your classes on time—incompletes are a pain in the butt.

* Know your school's policy on withdrawing from classes. Withdrawing from classes does not effect your GPA. Often you can withdraw up to one week before finals.

* Preview your prospective professors before you make your schedule. Get an idea of the work load they will require. Find out what kind of tests they give, how much reading they assign, and how much writing is required. Then decide if their classes will meet your needs. Play to your strengths.

* Stay current on who the good and bad professors are and why.

* Remember to take some classes just because you find them fun.

* Know your school's Pass/No-Pass policies. Many schools allow you to take classes Pass/No-Pass rather than for grades (A-F). If it exists, use this option wisely. For example, when you are taking an unusually heavy load, when you are particularly weak in the class, or when you simply are not interested in doing the work. Typically, the option is limited to courses not required for your major. Too many of P's tend to look bad on your transcripts. This is just as guess, but I think you could get by just fine with 8-10 P/NP classes on your record. Do not take my word on this, however. Ask some graduate admission people.

Playing the game is a creative process. These are just some of the features of the game to which to pay attention. The most important thing to remember is to **look for ways to make the system work for you.** This is the essence of being a *STUDENT*. Happy hunting!

TAKING TIME OFF

My advice is this: if you have another goal besides college you really want to pursue, great! Go for it! If you have nothing particular in mind, your best bet is to stay in school until you graduate.

GOING BACK TO SCHOOL

There's a lot of caca out there about how hard it is to return to school after you've taken time off. It is not true. Many of those who return to school usually do so with a greater sense of purpose. Most of them have experienced being adults, taking care of themselves, and improving their self-discipline. These all make schooling easier and more valuable in the long run. **My only suggestion to those returning to school is to take it easy at first, until you build up your learning skills.** Once your skills are up to it, do whatever you want.

NON-TRADITIONAL EDUCATION

Non-traditional education involves pursuing your degree in any manner other than the traditional university approach. Many schools offer a wide range of programs leading to a B.A. or B.S. that you can complete on your own time in a variety of ways which require little or no presence on a college campus. Typically these programs award credit for a variety of endeavors, including correspondence courses, seminars, workshops, private study, life experience, and others. Students enrolled in such programs are usually adults already in the workplace who would like to improve themselves through higher education. Typically these people have families and other obligations that preclude their attending a university full time.

This non-traditional approach to education is gaining wider and wider acceptance by the powers that be in our society, as the quality of the work one does becomes more important than the piece of paper one's degree is printed on. For example, people who have earned their masters degree in this manner have been accepted into Yale's doctoral program. And large companies such as IBM now support their employees' efforts to attain degrees through some non-traditional methods.

While it is true these degrees do not yet receive the broad acceptance of degrees from traditional schools, their acceptance is on the rise. It is also true that many organizations that offer non-traditional degrees are "degree factories" or fly-by-night operations. However, there are many more reputable institutes that provide opportunities for individuals who otherwise would not or could not earn their college degrees in the traditional manner. (One of these, the University of London, has been offering an extension program leading to a baccalaureate degree for more than 100 years.) Fortunately, there is a guide available that reviews and rates just about all the non-traditional programs throughout the world. Bear's Guide to Earning Non-Traditional College Degrees (John Bear, 1988, Ten Speed Press) is the best resource I know of for information on non-traditional undergraduate and graduate schooling. Dr. Bear is the leading authority on this form of education. If one is careful in choosing his or her program, **earning one's college degree in this manner can be a very rewarding experience.**

CHAPTER 10

GRADUATE SCHOOL:

HEAVEN AND / OR H . . .

Graduate school is the pinnacle of our educational system. A Ph.D. is the highest academic degree you can achieve. **Graduate school is also the arena where your skill as a** *STUDENT* **is most telling.** The more skilled *STUDENTS* have a great time in graduate school and complete their work considerably earlier than most of their peers. The less skilled students either go through hell and finish their work in the average amount of time (which, depending upon the field and the school, is between 5 and 7 years), take it a little easier and finish their work in twice the time it takes an average student, or in the worst cases, go through hell while taking twice as much time. In this chapter you will be provided with guidelines that can help you make graduate school a fun, rewarding, and relatively quick experience.

For those of you who are new to this game, we need to differentiate between two types of graduate programs: professional and academic. Academic programs are those that result in a Doctor of Philosophy (Ph.D.). Professional programs are those that lead to other Doctoral degrees, such as M.D. (Doctor of Medicine), D.D.S. (Doctor of Dental Science), and J.D. (Doctor of Jurisprudence). Master of Business Administration (M.B.A.) also falls in the professional degree category. Practically all other masters degrees are academic in the nature of their programs.

For the purposes of this discussion, the largest difference between academic and professional graduate programs is the way in which they are structured. **Professional programs are rigidly structured; academic programs are loosely structured.** In professional programs almost your entire course schedule is laid out for you. There are few electives available, and you usually have a fixed time in which to complete your work. Medical school is a 4-year program, plus a 1-year internship, plus a 2-year residency. Law School is a 3-year program.

M.B.A. programs typically take 2 years. Unless students are taking courses for programs in a non-traditional manner such as through correspondence or night school, students in these programs are expected, and often required, to compete their programs within these fixed times.

Academic programs are the antithesis of professional programs. **There are typically few required courses and there are many electives offered.** The number of courses required vary not only from discipline to discipline, but from program to program. One university psychology program may require its students to take five courses, while another school's psychology program may require twelve courses. Within these programs there are also few, if any, time constraints. At UCLA the average psychology graduate student completes the Ph.D. program in five to six years. However I know of one student that completed his work in two years, and another that completed his work in seventeen. **There are a great many opportunities to lengthen or shorten your stay in graduate school.**

Whether you choose an academic or professional program, the skills put forth throughout this book will serve you well. However, the rigidity of professional programs leave students with little room for strategic maneuvering. The loose structure of most academic programs, on the other hand, invites such movement. Hence, this chapter will be concerned with the tactics and strategies conducive to achieving success in a minimal amount of time in academic graduate programs.

GETTING IN

WHY GO?

There are two very fundamental reasons to get your doctorate:

1. Money
2. Choices

An average person with a doctorate can be expected to earn one and half times as much as a person with an undergraduate degree.   Perhaps more important, **the opportunities for a person with a doctorate are far greater, and more easily taken advantage of,** that for a person with an undergraduate degree. A doctorate will gain you entrance into all levels of academia: teaching, research, administration. Many doctoral degrees will also open doors in both private industry and government offices. If you have entrepreneurial leanings and have ideas to sell (such as a new approach to marketing or management training) a doctorate will at least get you heard. You may not agree with this, but it is a fact that the person with a Dr. in front of her name gets instant credibility in our society, as well as most other societies on the planet. This makes it much easier to accomplish your goals.

CHOOSING A GRADUATE SCHOOL

In general, the better the reputation of the school and the program—the better your reputation after you graduate. This is particularly true at the beginning of your career, when all people know about you is the school you came from. After you produce work, that work will speak for you much louder than the name of the school on your degree. Although a degree from Stanford will open more doors for you than a degree from Boise State University, **in the long run it is the individual who is actually more valuable that will earn the most.** In the end only academicians care about what school you went to, everybody else wants to know if you can deliver a valuable service, provide important results, or explain complex ideas competently. If you can, people will eventually not care where you went to school.

This being said let's look at three factors that you should take into account when deciding on a program:

1. **Interest match**
2. **Quality of program**
3. **Acceptance/completion policy**

INTEREST MATCH

Neither the quality of the department nor its acceptance/completion policy makes much difference if there is not at least one professor at the school with whom you're interested in working and vice-versa. We will talk in greater depth about this. For now suffice it to say **you need to choose a program with a few professors who are working in areas that interest you.** If you have a passion for twentieth-century literature, choosing a program which is primarily known for its Shakespearean and Medieval scholars would be a mistake. The chances of getting accepted are relatively slim, as admission committees are usually sensitive about the interest match between the applicants and the department. Furthermore, even if you do get in, finding a professor to be seriously interested in your work would be unlikely, and without such a professor's interest you may never get your degree. If you have a passion for a particular subject or approach, it is almost always in your best interests to find a program with professors who share that passion.

QUALITY OF PROGRAM

The quality of your discipline's program is defined by the resources available to it. This availability of resources is often reflected in that program's rank in comparison with other programs in that discipline. Resources fall into four categories: professors, research facilities, libraries, and money. **In the best programs you have the opportunity to work with the most accomplished professors, the most up-to-date research facilities, and the most complete libraries.** It's one thing to attend a school with one or two libraries, it's another thing completely to have seventeen libraries at your disposal. Believe me, it makes a difference. When I attended UCLA I had the second largest university library system in the country at my disposal (Harvard was #1). It was wonderful.

It should come as no surprise then, that the best programs are also those that are the most well endowed. **This is critical, as the more money there is in the program, the more money there is available for you.** This is not necessarily a reflection of the size or mystique of an institution. Often small, less prestigious universities have extremely prestigious and well funded individual programs, and vice-versa. Having all these resources at your disposal provides you with the opportunity for truly remarkable learning experience.

ACCEPTANCE/COMPLETION POLICY

There are two general attitudes schools have about acceptance into their programs. One attitude is: "**If a student is good enough to be accepted into our program, he is good enough to get his degree.**" The other attitude is: "**Only a percentage of those we admit are good enough to get their degrees.**" Programs with the "everyone succeeds" attitude will do everything they can to help their students succeed. The only way to get kicked out of these programs is to be both obnoxious and incompetent. Being just one or the other will most likely be excused. Programs with the "only the best succeed" policy look for students to drop from the program. They often set quotas such as dropping the bottom 20% of each class after the first year. Schools with the "everyone succeeds" policy foster cooperation and provide a much better work environment. Schools with the "only the best succeed" policy promote competition and pettiness. Find out the policy of the schools before you seriously consider them.

THE ADMISSIONS PROCESS

The admissions process for professional graduate programs is much the same as for undergraduate programs—by the numbers. Your GPA, MCAT, LSAT, or GMAT scores are what matter most to professional graduate programs. Exceptions are made, though they are few in number. When exceptions are made, they are usually a result of communication between a prospective student and someone on the admissions committee. Follow the guidelines in the previous chapter if you need alternatives to the standard admission process.

The admission process for academic graduate programs is an entirely different beast. This is due, primarily, to the different role of the graduate students in these programs. **In the sciences and social sciences the graduate students are not only students aiming to complete their Ph.D.'s, they are also assistants to their chosen professors, helping to advance their professors' work.** **In the humanities, though not actually working as assistants, graduate students are still expected to validate and support their professors' work.** This being the case, these programs are not only looking for the best students by the numbers, they are also looking for the best colleagues. Often a student with weaker numbers is accepted over a student with stronger numbers because a professor views that student as a better partner.

The admission process is generally a two-stage process. For the first cut, the admissions committee screens out the worst students and chooses a pool of acceptable applicants. Then, if one of the professors, because of a match in interests and/or personalities, wants to work with one of these applicants, s/he is accepted. The remaining positions are filled according to the numbers. This is why many students with excellent numbers do not get accepted into various graduate programs.

REQUIREMENTS

The standard requirements for entry into graduate programs, in order of importance, are as follows:

1. **Your Undergraduate GPA**
2. **Your GRE Scores (general and subject)**
3. **Your Statement of Purpose**
4. **Your Research/Performance Background**
5. **Your Letters of Recommendation**

Your GPA

The value of your undergraduate GPA speaks for itself. The higher, the better, particularly in your area of specialization. You will find it difficult to get in a graduate program the standard way with a GPA lower than 3.4, and all but impossible with a GPA of lower than 3.0 unless there is a mitigating cause or you showed steady academic improvement. For instance if your GPA was 3.8 during your last two years, but only a 2.0 before that, this points to you becoming more goal-oriented as you matured, and will often work in your favor.

Your GRE Scores

Your scores on the Graduate Record Exams (GREs) also speak for themselves. For those of you who are unfamiliar with these tests they come in two varieties: the general test and your subject test. Most programs require you to take both of these tests. The general GRE is much the same as the SAT. It is composed of verbal, math, and analytical sections. The subject GRE tests you on your knowledge of the specific field you intend to study. Like the SAT, you can take the GRE several times. Unlike the SAT, only certain parts of the GRE may matter. If you're applying to graduate programs in literature it is not unusual for them to disregard your scores on the math portion of the test. If you're considering programs in engineering, your math scores will obviously be heavily weighted. Take this into account as you prepare for these tests. When you are checking out potential graduate programs, **find out the average GPAs and GRE scores of the students that are actually admitted,** rather than the minimum scores required for admission, and see if you're in the ball park before applying.

Though you may take the GREs several times, note that when your scores are sent to the universities to which you apply—all your scores are sent.   Some schools will only consider your most recent scores, other schools will consider your best scores, still other schools will average all your scores. It is therefore in your best interest to be as well prepared for these tests as you can be. Take a few practice tests to see where you stand. (Practice tests can be found in your college or local bookstores.) If your scores need improving—get to work! For the general GRE, simply taking practice tests and reviewing your basic algebra and geometry will be all most of you need to do. For the subject GRE get out all your old flashcards and outlines and use them to prepare.   If you have outlines, flashcard them—the GRE is a multiple-choice test. If you don't have flashcards and outlines, reviewing an introductory textbook may suffice. When you review such a text, flashcard the information in each chapter and follow the guidelines in chapter 5 of this book. If this is not enough, there are a number of GRE preparation courses available to you. Inquire at your school counseling and testing office for the ones in your vicinity.

One final note on preparing for these tests: if you require a lot of preparation, take one test at a time. This will allow you concentrate your efforts on a smaller task, thus increasing your chances of achieving higher scores.

Your Statement of Purpose

Your statement of purpose is usually a 2-to-5 page paper which integrates where you've been with where you are going. In the statement you outline your academic interests and professional goals and what you have done to date in pursuit of them.   Unless you speak to members of the department personally, this is the way they judge whether or not you would fit into the program at their university (i.e., provide some professor with an interested contributor). **If you have done your homework, you will know about the research/writing interests of three or four professors in the area of your choice and will tailor your statement to their interests.** When writing your statement you need to strike a balance between having your interests be specific enough to allow the admissions committee to get a clear picture of where you might fit in, and broad enough so the committee can see you fitting into a number of places. Also, be sure you say something about your willingness to change and grow. Remember, your goal is to be a student, and part of your role as a student is to be shaped by your teacher.

Besides giving an indication of your interests, your statement of purpose enables members of the department to evaluate your writing ability. **Make sure your statement is well written, structurally as well as grammatically.** Get a competent editor to go over it with you—this can make a world of difference in your presentation.

Research/Performance Background

Depending on the discipline you choose to study at the graduate level, you will need either college-level research experience, for the sciences and the social sciences, or performing experience (usually writing) for the humanities. **In either case, it is to your great advantage if you have managed to publish one of your papers.** While it will not hurt you if you have not, it will help you a great deal if you have. If you do not have the appropriate research or writing background in your area—get it! Go to a university (preferably one where you are known) and offer your services as an assistant to a professor whose work seems interesting to you, or take a class which offers the kind of experience you need.

Your Letters of Recommendation

You will usually be asked to submit three letters of recommendation. The more prominent your recommenders are the better. Two or more of your letters should be from academicians in your area. Make sure they are enthusiastic. Graduate programs typically request that these recommendations be confidential, so before you have somebody commit to writing you a recommendation ask them what kind of recommendation they will write. Your strong recommenders will be glad to tell you. Some will even be happy to give you a copy of the recommendation they write. You need good recommendations. Believe me, **just about everyone who gets accepted has them.**

These are the standard requirements. If you have a 3.8 + GPA (from a top school), a 1500 general GRE score, a 750 subject GRE score, an exceptionally well written statement of purpose, excellent research/writing history, and glowing recommendations, you will be a lock for almost any position. A select few students fall into this category. The rest of you must take additional steps to assure yourselves entry into the programs of your choice.

THAT LITTLE SOMETHING EXTRA:
THE SECRET INGREDIENT

The question graduate admissions committees seek to answer is **"Which of these applicants can be one of us?"** Understand, they are looking for peers and people with whom they will enjoy working. If you have stellar GRE scores, a great GPA, etc. you will appear to be one of them, and you will be accepted. However, if your record isn't impeccable (and most students fit into this category), you will have to demonstrate in other ways that you can be one of them.

If your background is solid enough to make the first cut in a graduate admissions process, yet not outstanding enough to grant you automatic admission, here is what you can do to significantly increase your chances of acceptance:

Exercise 10.1 Improving your chances of getting into graduate school

1. *Narrow your list of schools down to four or five. You can choose more, if you're willing to do the work that follows.*

2. *Select one, possibly two, professors at each school whose work interests you. If no one's work at a particular school intrigues you, select another school.*

3. *Go to a good research library and read everything you can that each professor has written. Do any additional reading necessary (i.e., reading a particular novel he has written about) in order to be conversant in that professor's area of expertise.*

4. *Write a letter to each professor you have researched, expressing your interest in his/her current work and a desire to meet him/her.*

5. *Call him/her up to set up an appointment.*

6. *Visit with as many professors as you can and talk intelligently about their work. Get to know them and give them the opportunity to get to know*

you. It is not necessary to demonstrate your superiority regarding their work. You do not and will not know more about their area than they do. Your goals are simply to demonstrate you can be a contributing member to their research/writing efforts, and to make clear the connection between what they have accomplished and what you hope to accomplish during your graduate studies. In addition to making a strong impression, you will learn if this is a person you would enjoy working with.

If you are successful, when the time comes that professor will speak in support of your admission to the program. If your stats are at least in the ball park, in all likelihood you will be admitted. If you can't meet professors personally, establish a relationship by phone and/or letter. The best time to meet them is the summer or fall before you apply for admission to a program. If you wait until the applications are submitted, some professors, as a matter of policy, will not meet with you. They may feel it inappropriate to meet with prospective students once the review process has started.

If your background is not solid enough to make the first cut, you have your work cut out for you. Here is where you find out how badly you want your Ph.D. **Somehow you must show a group of scholars you can be one of them.** One alternative is to get into a masters program, perform at a high level, then apply to a school's doctoral program. Many STUDENTS follow this route. If your background isn't strong enough to get into a masters program, you may still take graduate-level classes at most universities without being formally accepted into their programs. If, through your work in these classes, you shine, you stand a good chance of being formally accepted. If this option does not appeal to you, you will have to get seriously creative.

The best approach to use at this point is to actually to be a scholar: be one of them, do what they do. You will have to do some significant reading, research, and writing on your own. **In essence, you will have to do your own graduate work.** By the way, this work could be a lot of fun and it could be extremely rewarding. You could travel and do cross-cultural studies. You could test industrial psychological theories in a business in which you are involved. You could write a novel. Whatever you do, it will take great initiative. It may be possible to find a professor at some local school who will help guide your efforts. If your work is good enough, you will have demonstrated your ability to do high-level academic work. You will also have done something few graduate students do, thus making yourself stand out even more. You will then stand a good chance of getting into a doctoral program somewhere.

Finally, if you believe you have the background and are still not accepted, reapply the next year. Many students do not get accepted the first time around (I was one of them). If this is the case, find out why you were rejected, then fix it. Fixing it might include applying to some different, perhaps less prestigious schools. It might include getting more research behind you. It might be a matter of adjusting your statement of purpose to suit a particular department. Most likely it will involve getting to know the right people. Regardless, in the ensuing months between applications, do work that demonstrates the seriousness of your intent. **If you really want your Ph.D.— you can get it!**

FINANCING YOUR GRADUATE EDUCATION

Financing your graduate education can be very different from financing your undergraduate education (especially at many of the larger institutions). **Graduate students often fund all or part of their education through research and/or teaching assistantships.** The amount each school pays its graduate assistants varies greatly from school to school, and sometimes from department to department. In psychology departments at some schools, teaching assistants will make upward of $1,300/mo. and at others they will only make $350/mo. The quality and size of an institution goes a long way towards determining what that institution pays its assistants. Usually, the larger the university, the higher the pay for assistantships. There are also fellowships (research and otherwise), scholarships, and a host of grants and loans available to graduate students. **Many schools go out of their way to insure that their graduate students are well taken care of.** Check with the people at the schools in which you are interested to find out what is available. This is not the whole story. Please refer to this heading in the previous chapter to help you continue your search for sources of money for your education.

GETTING OUT

Once you have gotten accepted to a graduate program, the next issue, is how do you have a great time while you're there? This is followed by, how do you get out in a timely manner? For most of us these issues seem to be related. **Usually, the faster and more efficiently a student does his/her work, the better experience s/he has.** Ph.D. programs are notorious for taking years and years for students to complete. Many student become so discouraged after several years they just quit and never complete their work. Graduate school does not have to be this way. It can be a fun and rewarding experience! There are three factors that will determine both how fast you proceed through your graduate education and how much work you ultimately do, and therefore how much fun you have. Obviously the less work you have to do, the faster you move and the more time you have for play. These factors are

1. Your choice of an advisor
2. The work you choose to do
3. Your organization and self-discipline

CHOOSING THE RIGHT ADVISOR

This is one of the most critical decisions you will make in your graduate education. A bad advisor can add three or more years of hell to your work. **A good advisor can help you earn your degree with alacrity and can contribute to your having a wonderful time.** Earlier I spoke about the relationship between advisor (professor) and student, the student being expected to help her advisor and vice-versa. Advisors can be loosely placed in one of two categories based upon how they view this trade off:

1. **those that consider graduate students to be slaves (particularly in the sciences and social sciences); those that view graduate students as bothersome pests they'd just as soon not have to deal with (particularly in the humanities)**
2. **those that consider the advisor/student relationship to be an interdependent one in which both parties support each other's efforts**

I suppose it is possible to add a third category, the advisor who sincerely believes he is there solely to support the graduate students. If this type exists they are few and far between. Which type of advisor you have goes a long way to determining the quality of graduate life you experience.

You can lose a lot of time having the wrong type of advisor. The two most common ways a bad advisor can get in your way are

1. **using you only to further their own careers**
2. **not caring about your work, seeing helping you as a chore**

Graduate school is rife with examples of both of these. I will provide you with one of each.

During their first year in the UCLA doctoral program in psychology, all students are required to do one research project. This is actually a practice project—results aren't important. The goal of this project is to give the first year students a chance to get their feet wet designing, running, analyzing, and reporting their own research. Typically, the result is a 20-30 page paper with 20-30 references. Students do the work under the guidance of their advisors. A friend of mine had the misfortune of having an advisor (who, by the way, was not tenured), who was seeking to both impress his peers with how tough he was on his students and get a publication out of his student's work. **Instead of the "practice project" my friend should have done, his advisor had him read well over 100 articles and books, and write a publishable 40-50 page paper. He must have done three times the work of most of his peers.**

Another friend of mine was in the process of deciding on her dissertation topic. She had spent a lot of time reading and doing pilot research to reach her decision. Her advisor was not interested in helping her during this process and took little interest in her work. In other words her advisor refused to advise her. **Only after she was finished and needed his approval, did he tell her that her ideas were not suitable. He denied approval of her work, and told her to come up with another idea. About six months of work went down the tubes.** A good advisor would have been working with her from the beginning, giving her the guidance she needed.

Guidelines you should consider in selecting your advisor include:

* **Tenure**
* **Reputation**
* **Healthy cynicism**
* **Connections**
* **Affinity**

TENURE

Your advisor must be tenured, and preferably be a full professor. This is absolutely critical. There are two egregious problems with untenured advisors. First, they are highly likely to be heavily focused on their own careers. Whether they believe you are there to serve them or not, they usually **need** your work. They want tenure and so are seeking the approval of their peers. Usually they are tougher than they need to be. They will also be wanting you to publish so they can add to their quotas. (Professors often get credit as second authors on their students' work, and most of them should. There are, however, professors that unethically take credit as the first author on the work of their students. Be wary!) This is pressure and work you do not need. The decision to publish should be yours. Second, if during your stay, your untenured advisor is denied tenure, he/she will likely leave the school, leaving you without an advisor. In order to get another professor interested in working with you, you may have to change your work entirely. This can result in trashing two or three years worth of work.

For those of you who do not know, professors at research universities get tenure, as well as advancement, by publishing. The more they publish the greater chance they have to receive tenure and move up the professorial ladder. Full professors are generally better than associate professors in that they have advanced as far as they can and are typically more relaxed about the whole process. Assistant professors are not tenured. **In general, you should look for an advisor who is happy and content where s/he is.** You may find such a professor at any level, though more often than not they will be full professors.

In a few cases you may also need to take into account the age of the professor you are considering working with. When a professor is getting on in years and closing in on retirement, you need to find out if they will be around for the four to six years you will likely need to complete your work. Sometimes after losing his/her advisor to retirement, a graduate student will having to change his/her research when starting over again with a new advisor. Though not a common occurrence, it is not unheard of.

REPUTATION

Look for an advisor with a reputation for moving his/her students along at a good pace. At every university there are advisors whose students typically take longer or shorter times to complete their work. You will find advisors whose students usually take seven years to complete a four-year program as well as those whose students typically take four years or less. Usually this is a reflection of the advisor's work habits, not the individual students'. Whenever I handed my advisor work to be reviewed or edited, I received it back within a week. I know of advisors that would keep their students' work for three to four months before they got around to dealing with it. This is a common practice among many professors. It could add years to your work. Before selecting an advisor—check out their work habits. You may save yourself a lot of time and money.

HEALTHY CYNICISM

Your advisor should be just a little cynical about the whatever field she is in. **She shouldn't take it too seriously.** For while academia has certainly made its contributions to our society, only a small percentage of these contributions have been earth-shattering. Academia is not the be-all and end-all of life. **It will behoove you to have an advisor who has a life (preferably an enjoyable one) outside of his lab and office.** Often, though not always, these advisors are older men and women with a larger perspective on life. I've known a few young ones too. Either way they are usually wiser than most of their colleagues and a lot more fun to be around. A brief example:

While at UCLA in 1989 we had a recently emigrated Soviet psychologist give a presentation of his work. My advisor (as well as myself) was astounded that after four days on campus all the faculty talked about with this man was his work. Here we had a man who had personally experienced many of the sweeping changes occurring in eastern Europe and all people could talk about was the relation of Einsteinian and Lorentzian motion to perception. I personally had the opportunity to spend two hours discussing travel and the changes in the Soviet Union with him. He was fascinating. He was a wonderful man with a great heart. Few of my colleagues took the time to find that out.

CONNECTIONS

Depending on the type of work you plan to do after graduating, the connections your advisor has may or may not be important. If you are intending to pursue a career in academia, the more substantial a name your advisor has in her field, the more weight her recommendations will carry. Obviously, this is to your benefit. The same, of course, goes for other areas of endeavor. Many students select their advisors solely on that advisor's name value. These students assume that the bigger the name the better. This assumption is not always accurate. Although many big-name academicians make wonderful advisors, many others make lousy ones. Some of them do not have time for the many graduate students who want to work with them. Others have poor interpersonal skills. Still others have such large egos that they cannot allow their students to grow and flourish. **Before you decide to work with someone simply because they are well known—check them out.** If they are less than strong advisors, yet will be heavy-weight recommenders in a field in which you intend to work, you have an interesting decision to make. It's a trade-off that I advise you to evaluate carefully.

AFFINITY

A final, and important, factor to consider is the affinity between you and your prospective advisor. Do you get along? Do you like each other? Do you like his work? Is it the kind of work you can support?   Will he support your work? Remember, you will be working with this person closely for a number of years, and believe me, **your experience will be much more enjoyable if you and your advisor like and respect one another.**

CHOOSING THE RIGHT WORK

SELECTING YOUR DISSERTATION TOPIC.

Regardless of the discipline you chose, there are both express routes and scenic routes to getting your doctorate. **The type of work you choose goes a long way towards determining the route you will follow.** Different disciplines require different workloads and various amounts of time to accomplish them. Most Ph.D. programs have a variety of requirements—required course work, elective course work, language requirements, etc. All Ph.D. programs require you to do a dissertation. A dissertation is a substantial original work that contributes to your field of study. It is usually a piece of original research. If your goal is to complete a program in as little time as possible, there are some guidelines you should follow when deciding on your dissertation topic.

The best way to approach selecting a dissertation topic is to do so with your advisor. You want to find a topic that is interesting to him as well as you so he will be motivated to help you along. The more interested your advisor is in the topic, the more motivated he will be to help you along. Optimally your work will either contribute to or build upon his. This makes for a productive partnership.

DOING GOOD WORK — FAST

Your dissertation research will be expedited if you will follow these guidelines when setting it up:

* KISS
* **Win—Regardless of the outcome of your research**
* **Collect data in groups whenever possible.**

KISS: KEEP IT SIMPLE STUPID!

The simpler the research the better. **Simple research is elegant research.** Always keep your goal in mind: To get your Ph.D. In the humanities, choose to analyze one writer rather than one period. Even better, choose to analyze one work of one writer rather than his complete body of work. **Keep your focus as tight as you can.** Also, it is to your advantage to choose a topic which has not been written on by many other scholars. The less information you have to sift through, the less time it will take you to do your dissertation. In the sciences and social sciences this may mean working in relatively untapped areas in which little previous work has been done. **The less work that has come before you, the less work you have to review.**

Remember, you don't have to do great, important work to get your doctorate. Many students waste years attempting to do mind-blowing research. To paraphrase my advisor: "Get

your doctorate, then they will pay you to do mind-blowing research." You see, mind-blowing research doesn't often pan out. If you're getting paid, that's OK; you'll try again and still collect your paycheck. If you're a student, you're the one supplying the money and the time. Limit your research to something you can do in about a year, with a high likelihood of success. Remember, hardly any great scientists, great historians, great literary critics, etc. made their most important discoveries when they were in graduate school.

WIN —
REGARDLESS OF THE OUTCOME OF YOUR RESEARCH

Make sure you can win—regardless of the outcome of your research. **This means setting up your research so that you have something to contribute regardless of the result.** You can do this if you're motivated to do so. One of the biggest stops in the graduate process in the sciences and social sciences is research that doesn't work as hypothesized. Often students have to start over from square one. If, however, you design your project so that any result is significant, you will often be able to proceed with your dissertation no matter what happens. This, by the way, is the acid test of the best students. The best students set up events so that they either win, or they win. Doing so can save you years of work.

COLLECT DATA IN GROUPS WHENEVER POSSIBLE

In the social sciences, particularly in psychology and sociology, **set up your research so you can collect your data in groups.** This is so important that in most cases if I could not see my way to doing this I would change my topic. Taking years to collect data is not unheard of, yet with the right experimental design, you can get your data in weeks. Not only will this expedite your work, it will protect you against mistakes by keeping your costs to a minimum. I know one student who collected survey data one subject at a time. After he had collected data from 72 subjects, he found he had to redo three of the survey questions. Seventy-two hours of work done over three months was wasted. It is not uncommon for graduate students to lose a year of work in this manner. You want your mistakes to be as inexpensive as possible. I also know a student who was able to collect data, 20 subjects at a time, on approximately 450 subjects in five weeks. His work went very, very, smoothly.

YOUR ORGANIZATION AND DISCIPLINE

ORGANIZATION

To earn your doctoral degree, you will have to take classes and make an original contribution to your field. **The more you can make the work you do in class contribute to your dissertation, the less work you will ultimately end up doing. Similarly, the more you can make the work you do outside of class contribute to your dissertation the faster and smoother your journey will go.** Often this takes some ingenuity, but it has the potential of saving you years of time and therefore money. It's worth the price.

DISCIPLINE

Graduate school is very different from college. It provides you with opportunity upon opportunity to procrastinate. Often, there are no deadlines. What deadlines there are can usually be extended endlessly. If you do not want to write on a particular day, you don't have to. Additionally, you are provided with many opportunities to do others' work which won't directly contribute to your degree. Keep this work to a minimum. **You will do best if you treat graduate school like a job. Plan to work 8 hours per day 5 days per week. Make sure you leave yourself two or three days where you only work on your own dissertation-orientated projects.** If you do this, you'll find yourself progressing steadily toward your goal while still having time for relationships, entertainment, travel, and fun.

NON-TRADITIONAL

GRADUATE EDUCATION

As with undergraduate programs, there are non-traditional graduate programs, at both the M.A. and Ph.D. levels. These programs are a boon to adult learners who want to further their education and/or improve their earning potential. These programs make higher education possible for those of us who have responsibilities (such as families and careers) we can't simply set aside for the two to seven years it would take to get an advanced degree by the traditional route. Students in these programs find an advisor (one who holds a Ph.D. in their area of interest) and work with her in much the same manner they would if they were in a traditional program. The key difference being that they work when and where it is most convenient for them. Again, if you think you might be interested in exploring such programs, I highly recommend Bear's Guide to Earning Non-Traditional College Degrees (John Bear, 1988, Ten Speed Press) as a good place to start.

RANDOM TIPS ON PLAYING THE GAME

ON SELECTING YOUR
DISSERTATION COMMITTEE

Dissertation committees are typically comprised of five members of the university's faculty: Your advisor—the chairman of your committee, your secondary advisor—a professor who has contributed to your work, and three other professors—often none of whom has made any significant contribution to your dissertation. Of these other three it is common that two of them come from outside your department. These five professors are the people who will ultimately graduate you. In most programs, you choose them yourself. When choosing them, follow similar guidelines to the ones outlined for advisors. **You want committee members who are there to support your efforts and to offer constructive criticism.**

When things go awry, it is often because some insecure bozo, who really hasn't as clue as to what you're doing, decides he wants to show off his dubious power by requesting that you alter your work. Things can also go wrong when egos on your committee clash. Stories abound of graduate students getting caught in the crossfire between two of their committee members, resulting in students having to go through contortions to satisfy diametrically opposing views in their dissertations. Though these wars are usually involve the chairman and some other committee member, they are brought about by the carelessness of the student. **When selecting your committee, be certain that the members are in fundamental agreement with the relevant positions of both you and your advisor.** If your advisor is a cognitive psychologist, don't ask a staunch, died-in-the-wool behaviorist to sit on your committee. It is best to save yourself the trouble by selecting committee members for their ability to support, rather than for some other criteria such as "name." If you have a good advisor, consult with her before all appointments.

In keeping with the above—**get competent at judging character. The better you can read people the smoother your journey.** If you haven't got a clue how to judge who will be supportive of you—find an ally who does. Once you have selected your committee, keep them abreast of your progress. You will hopefully be in close contact with your advisor—she will evaluate all your work. Some of the other members will be interested in your work as it progresses. If they are, meet with them periodically to get their feedback. If they have any concerns, you will often be able to address them before your oral exams, thus increasing the chances that your oral evaluation will proceed smoothly.

ON TAKING ORAL EXAMS

During your graduate studies you will almost certainly have to take oral exams. Depending on the program, you may have to take as many as three of them. Orals are of three general types: comprehensive orals, orals for the preliminary defense of your dissertation, and orals for the final defense of your dissertation.

During your comprehensive orals you're tested on your knowledge of your field. These are usually combined with a written exam. **During your preliminary defense orals, you present and defend your plan for your dissertation.** It is usually at this point that most students find out if they are going to run into trouble. This is where your committee has the greatest opportunity to "suggest" changes and additions to your work. For example, they could ask you to read and analyze three more of an author's works, or they could ask you to run added experiments. They could even ask you to change your whole experimental design. These "improvements" can add a year or more to your work. If, however, you have been in good communication with your committee members prior to these orals, you will have significantly diminished the chances of being asked to make major changes in your work.

During your final defense of your dissertation you present and defend your completed dissertation. Sometimes final defenses are just rubber stamps and are not taken too seriously. Other times they are quite formal and taken very seriously. Here too, committee members can ask you to make changes, changes that can often be avoided by remaining in good communication with your committee members throughout the process. It is not uncommon for a committee member to ask you to rewrite parts of your dissertation or add a chapter. The conventions of each individual program determines how final defenses are viewed.

There are other steps you can take to improve the likelihood that your orals go the way you want them to. First, do good work. Also do the right work. **If your work is close to you're advisor's heart, it will be in his best interests to insure that all proceeds smoothly, as your work is a reflection of his own.** Stay in close contact with your advisor—he can help you navigate a smooth path. Select the right committee members and stay in close enough contact with them so that you are able to handle their concerns early in the process.

Understand the true purpose of these exams. These exams are the last and best chance professors will have to determine if you are indeed one of them. **The true purpose of these exams** is to give you a chance to prove you belong in the fraternity. On one level they are really nothing more than a hazing. On another level they are a test to see if you can withstand the heat of presenting your work to your peers, a task you will be expected to perform many times during your academic career. **If you present your work and handle the ensuing questions and challenges confidently—you're in.** In some sense your committee's job is to try to shake your confidence. If you do not appear confident members may jump on you. It is often in the face of such apparent lack of confidence that changes and additions are asked for.

The key, then, to taking oral exams is this: present your work and handle the challenges confidently. Most challenges are open-ended with no "right" answer. What you say in response to these challenges is rarely as important as how you say it. Remember, **you know more about your particular topic than everyone you will be facing, with the possible exception of your advisor,** and she should be your strongest supporter. You are the expert. Respectfully treat these people as students, and take the role of the teacher. **The more confident and self-possessed you appear, the fewer challenges there will be, the smoother your oral will go, and the more fun you will have.**

ON GRADES

In doctoral programs grades barely matter. Your research and writing is what's most important. The rule is that "you need B's to pass." The corollary is that "Just about everybody gets B's." Grades matter somewhat more in the "only the best survive" programs. In the "everyone succeeds" programs they matter hardly at all. In almost every instance, if you do the work—you'll pass.

ON GETTING YOUR RESEARCH DONE

When doing your research in the sciences and social sciences use undergraduate assistants whenever possible to help you tabulate data and run subjects. They are often loaded with ideas and will free up your time for your writing.

ON GETTING A MASTER'S DEGREE

If you only want a master's degree, and you can get into a Ph.D. program, do so. Since the end result of a Ph.D. program is a Ph.D., much less work is often required for a master's than in a terminal master's program. In a terminal master's program, the thesis is often expected to be a major work (usually about 60-80 pages), demonstrating mastery of some field. A typical "master's thesis" in the Ph.D. program in psychology at UCLA, such as it was, was the first year practice research project and write up—usually a simple 20-30 page effort. Another advantage of this route is that it gives you more options. Not only is it easier to continue on to the Ph.D., getting a master's this way is much, much less work. Typically Ph.D. programs require those that are admitted with an MA or MS to redo much of their past work.

ON THE U.S. POSTAL SERVICE

Mail all your correspondence during the admissions process using certified mail. It's a good habit to get into. This way both you and a department knows whether something was sent to them and received.

ON "LIFE, THE UNIVERSE, AND EVERYTHING"

Have a life—maintain your balance. Graduate school is only one part of existence. The journey is a lot more fun when you have interests and relationships unrelated to your work. Remember your other goals and nurture yourself. Of greatest import:

HAVE FUN !

APPENDIX: LIST OF EXERCISES

INDEX

Order Form

Please send me _____ copies of Easy A's: Winning the School Game. (Specify number of copies)

Cost:
   Book: $9.95 per book +
   Shipping: (Circle which method of shipment you prefer)
   Book rate: $2.00 for the first book and 75 cents for each additional
            book. (Allow two to four weeks for delivery)
   Air mail: $3.50 per book

Name:_____

Address:_____

City:_____ State: _____ Zip: _____

Mail Check or Money Order to:
                    Uptone Press
                    P.O.Box 82993
                    Portland, Oregon 97282

I understand that I may return this book for any reason, no questions asked, and receive a full refund as long as the book is returned in marketable condition.

Order Form

Please send me _____ **copies of Easy A's: Winning the School Game.** (Specify number of copies)

Cost:
   Book: $9.95 per book +
   Shipping: (Circle which method of shipment you prefer)
      Book rate: $2.00 for the first book and **75 cents** for each additional
            book. (Allow two to four weeks for delivery)
      Air mail: **$3.50** per book

Name:_____

Address:___ _____

City:_____ State: _____ Zip: _____

Mail Check or Money Order to:
                     Uptone Press
                     P.O.Box 82993
                     Portland, Oregon 97282

I understand that I may return this book for any reason, no questions asked, and receive a full refund as long as the book is returned in marketable condition.

Order Form

Please send me _____ copies of Easy A's: Winning the School Game. (Specify number of copies)

Cost:
  Book: $9.95 per book +
  Shipping: (Circle which method of shipment you prefer)
  Book rate: $2.00 for the first book and **75 cents** for each additional
            book. (Allow two to four weeks for delivery)
  Air mail: $3.50 per book

Name:_____

Address:_____

City:_____ State: _____ Zip: _____

Mail Check or Money Order to:
                    Uptone Press
                    P.O.Box 82993
                    Portland, Oregon 97282

I understand that I may return this book for any reason, no questions asked, and receive a full refund as long as the book is returned in marketable condition.

Order Form

Please send me _____ copies of Easy A's: Winning the School Game. (Specify number of copies)

Cost:
  Book: $9.95 per book +
  Shipping: (Circle which method of shipment you prefer)
    Book rate: $2.00 for the first book and 75 cents for each additional book. (Allow two to four weeks for delivery)
  Air mail: $3.50 per book

Name:_____

Address:_____

City:_____ State: _____ Zip: _____

Mail Check or Money Order to:
              Uptone Press
              P.O.Box 82993
              Portland, Oregon 97282

I understand that I may return this book for any reason, no questions asked, and receive a full refund as long as the book is returned in marketable condition.

Order Form

Please send me _____ copies of Easy A's: Winning the School Game. (Specify number of copies)

Cost:
   Book: $9.95 per book +
   Shipping: (Circle which method of shipment you prefer)
     Book rate: $2.00 for the first book and 75 cents for each additional
           book. (Allow two to four weeks for delivery)
     Air mail: $3.50 per book

Name:_____

Address:_____

City:_____ State:_____ Zip:_____

Mail Check or Money Order to:
          Uptone Press
          P.O.Box 82993
          Portland, Oregon 97282

I understand that I may return this book for any reason, no questions asked, and receive a full refund as long as the book is returned in marketable condition.